THE LORD
IS MY COUNSEL

THE LORD IS MY COUNSEL

* * *

A BUSINESSMAN'S
PERSONAL EXPERIENCES WITH THE BIBLE

by

MARION E. WADE

with

GLENN D. KITTLER

PRENTICE
HALL
PRESS

New York   London   Toronto   Sydney   Tokyo   Singapore

The poem "Questionable Progress," which appears on page 43, was written by Steven Schlitzer. It is reprinted from THE LINK, copyright 1963 by the General Commission on Chaplains and Armed Forces Personnel, and used by permission.

PRENTICE HALL PRESS
15 Columbus Circle
New York, NY 10023

This special edition published
by Prentice Hall Press,
a division of Simon & Schuster, Inc.
Previously published by Prentice-Hall, Inc.

PRENTICE HALL PRESS and colophons are
registered trademarks of Simon & Schuster, Inc.

Library of Congress Catalog Card Number: 66-19885

T54065

Manufactured in the United States of America

25 24 23 22

This book is dedicated to the memory of my mother, who brought me to a saving knowledge of the Lord Jesus Christ by asking the most important question ever put to me—"Marion, don't you want to become a Christian?"

My response lies in these pages.

INTRODUCTION

You should meet Marion Wade. Through the years that I have known him, my heart is always made stronger and courage rises higher when we meet.

From time immemorial men have met in the marketplace to exchange their wares and their views. They do so today in the most remote and primitive places in the heart of New Guinea, for example, and in the sophisticated and highly sensitive Stock Exchange in New York City. The material needs and desires of men are met in the marketplace, as well as answers to some intellectual problems. But what about matters of the spirit?

Integrity is indispensable in the dealings of men with each other. Always there have been rascals in business so that both buyer and seller have had to be alert to the possibility of dishonesty. In the long run, however, honesty is not only the best policy; it is the only policy.

Integrity is based more upon the heart than the head of man. It has a spiritual foundation, whether recognized or not. There are those who have faced squarely their own heart, as well as their fellowmen, and have found God to be indispensable in the marketplace as well as in the home and the church.

Marion Wade is one such person, a man's man, and God's man. He is a successful man of business and of the Book that gives meaning and motivation to him. What book? Sir Walter Scott's servant asked that question when his master asked for the Book. "There is only one Book," replied the elderly man of letters. "The Bible."

Marion Wade believes ardently and enthusiastically in the Bible, with its freedom for the human spirit, and in the free market. Both are indispensable for free men.

This outstanding man of the marketplace with his keen insight and down-to-earth common sense has many valuable lessons to share with us of this generation in its uncertainties, both material and spiritual. Meet Marion E. Wade in these pages.

Dr. V. Raymond Edman
Chancellor, Wheaton College
Wheaton, Illinois

CONTENTS

THE LORD
IS MY COUNSEL

THE LITTLE BLACK BOOK

If today I applied for an executive position with the company of which I am Chairman of the Board of Directors, I wouldn't even be granted an interview. My application form would be dismally brief. Before going into my present business I played semiprofessional baseball for a few years. I sold insurance for a few years, and I sold aluminumware for a few more years, none of which would make me of particular value to a thriving corporation. Moreover, I couldn't boast of a college degree, not even a high school diploma, and my record in grammar school wouldn't mark me as the one most likely to succeed. Though I started the company myself, I had no business experience or acumen which might have given me the slightest hope that it would one day become the leader in its field. I didn't even think of that; I was merely trying to earn a living during the worst period of America's economic history. Despite my personal shortcomings and the company's hazardous beginnings, the fact remains that ServiceMaster has thrived and today I find myself at the head of a multi-million-dollar, international corporation. And yet this fact is not as important to me as the way it has all come about.

The head of any corporation big or small has the responsibility of conducting his business along lines that will keep his employees working and keep his stock-holders happy. But this is not his first responsibility. His first responsibility is to conduct his business along lines that will be pleasing to the Lord. And he must do so not because of any rewards he hopes to receive but because, for a Christian, there is no other way.

Many of the men I meet in business are ready to declare that they are Christians if the subject comes up in our conversations. On the other hand, few of them have been able to state that they are applying their religious convictions to their business affairs. Either it hasn't occurred to them that they should or they haven't figured out how they could. In many cases, these men feel that by attending church on Sundays and perhaps even participating in Bible classes they are fulfilling all of their Christian obligations. The simple fact is that Christian obligations are also Christian privileges. They encompass the whole man. If there is any area of a professed Christian's activities which is not permeated by Christian convictions, then a very important part of that person's spiritual existence has yet to come alive.

It is also a simple fact that the spiritual gap in the

life of many a Christian businessman is his business itself. At one time this gap was regarded merely as one of the occupational hazards of the business world— loving your enemies and turning your other cheek were all right in Sunday School, but in the marketplace they meant bankruptcy. In recent years, however, the American business community has grown increasingly aware that its internal strength and its influence on the American way of life have been threatened by a moral bankruptcy at all levels, a threat so serious that the freedom which business needs in order to survive has been steadily curtailed by government controls. When there is an internal problem in any kind of community, it cannot be solved just by sending in Federal troops. The problem has to be resolved by the people who comprise that community. It follows, then, that the moral bankruptcy which has made words like price-fixing, kick-backs and payola part of the business vocabulary has to be overcome within the business community, each businessman starting with himself.

The job has already begun. Business organizations like the American Management Association have, for the past few years, sponsored seminars at which business ethics are discussed. Thus far, the most important aspect of these conferences is that they are being held; business leaders are recognizing that the way they do business is as critical as whether business is bad or good. This is a step in the right direction primarily because it acknowledges the role of morality in business decisions. But the situation is much more basic than that, and this was excellently illustrated at an American Management Association conference a few years ago when, after listening for hours to discussions on business ethics, the representative of a large corporation got up and said: "Gentlemen, whenever I have to make a decision involving ethics I simply consult the little black book that can be found in every hotel room."

That is the heart of the matter. For too long, the business community has been using the word "ethics" as a euphemism for morality, for religion, for God. Perhaps the reason for trying to dodge the issue is that facing it would burden a man with far more responsibility for his business conduct than he cares to accept. But dodging the issue doesn't change the facts. The executive who calls himself a Christian is obligated to conduct his business in a Christian way or he is not a Christian. It is as simple as that. At the same time, the executive who is truly Christian has the spiritual privilege of knowing that God's guidance is available to him at all times through God's book—the Bible.

Prayer, someone once said, is man speaking to God, and the Bible is God speaking to man. Many people seem to be aware of this to some extent. It is common knowledge, for example, that the Bible is consistently America's best-selling book year after year, and presumably it is being read by those who buy it or receive it as a gift. True, in places it is a difficult book to read. The

Old Testament, particularly, contains references to people and events that require a solid background in history to understand, and it is therefore a good idea for the person beginning to study the Bible to do some supplementary ancient history reading as well. However, the person who regards the Bible merely as history is depriving himself of its great treasures.

The Bible is a practical guide to Christian living. It contains the Lord's counsel for all the problems that face us, and it is addressed to those who are specifically seeking that counsel. The Bible deals with spiritual affairs and its glorious messages can be grasped only by men who understand spiritual things, who are themselves of the Spirit. Clearly, then, until a man is willing to accept the Bible as the Word of God and is ready to be reborn in Christ as a child of the Lord, the words of the Bible will be meaningless to him and he will never learn how to put the Book to its proper use.

There is a story, perhaps apocryphal, involving Yogi Berra and Hank Aaron during a World Series game between the New York Yankees and the Milwaukee Braves. As usual, Yogi was keeping up his ceaseless chatter, intended both to pep up his teammates and to distract the Milwaukee batters. Aaron came up, and as he stood there waiting for the pitch, Yogi tried to divert his attention by saying: "You're holding the bat wrong, Henry. You should hold it so that you can read the trademark." Henry said nothing, but he promptly hit the next pitch into the left-field bleachers. After tagging up at home plate, Aaron looked at Berra and said: "I didn't come up here to read."

Just as Hank Aaron knew what his bat was for, so does the true Christian know what the Bible is for. He knows that God did not create man and then abandon him to stumble his way through history without divine guidance. To be sure, God does communicate directly with men, Spirit to spirit, but it would be presumptuous for a man to count on having his own "hot line" to God over which to receive last minute instructions whenever he faces some crisis. God has already spoken His mind, He has revealed it to the Bible writers, and these instructions of His are most effective when they have been learned by regular Bible reading long before the "last minute."

Periodically, our country suffers business and political scandals which hit the front pages and shame us all. Also periodically, respected business and political leaders suggest that committees of prominent citizens be appointed to compose a new code of ethics for our time. As worthy as this seems at first, it is actually superfluous. We don't need a new code of ethics. We need only abide by the instructions for moral conduct given to us by God in the Bible. For that matter, morality cannot be negotiated, it cannot be legislated, it cannot be revamped by men to meet the circumstances of any time or any place. From the beginning of time, morality has been as constant and unchanging as God Himself.

Whenever men have taken a step forward in any sphere of morality, whether in business, social justice or human relations, it wasn't because somebody thought up a new law but rather because somebody thought of returning to the old law, the Law of God as defined in the Word of God—the Bible.

I don't expect anybody but a dedicated atheist to disagree with this, but I am disquieted by the fact that many of the people who agree with me do so only passively. As I do business with a man, I learn something about his convictions, and this is important. I feel that when I know what a man believes I can get a better idea of how he behaves. There have been times, however, when I had the impression I was in the presence of another believer, only to have the man turn into a snarling tiger when it came to agreeing on terms or carrying out the terms we had agreed upon.

This leads to an inescapable fact: *If you don't live it, you don't believe it.*

The difficulty seems to be either in the refusal or the inability of some people to realize that man is a spiritual as well as a physical creature and that he is spiritually (morally) responsible for the way he conducts himself in the physical (material) aspect of his life. A man is as accountable to God for his stewardship in the ministry of business as much as in the ministry of being a husband or a father. "Woe is me if I preach not the Gospel," Paul wrote to the Corinthians, and by this he did not only mean preaching in a pulpit: he meant the preaching each of us performs in the way we conduct ourselves in our daily affairs, and we can preach either the Gospel of God or the gospel of man.

There can be no halfway measures in this, or we become like the boy who was climbing a tree one day, lost his grip and began to fall. "God, save me!" he cried. Partway down, a thick branch caught him by the breeches and held him fast, and he said: "Never mind, God, I'm okay now. I don't need you."

We always need God. We can never rely solely on our own opinions, our own judgments, in deciding what is the right thing to do. No committee of mere men can produce an effective moral code for today's world unless it is based on the moral instructions God gave the world thousands of years ago, instructions which are just as applicable today as they were the day they were first written down.

The Psalmist wrote: "Thy word is a lamp unto my feet, and a light unto my path. I have sworn and I will perform it, that I will keep thy righteous judgments. . . . Thy testimonies have I taken as an heritage for ever: for they are the rejoicing of my heart. I have inclined mine heart to perform thy statutes alway, even unto the end." (Psalm 119:105, 106, 111, 112).*

And Peter wrote the Christians in Asia Minor: "The word of the Lord endureth forever. And this is the word which by the gospel is preached unto you." (I Pet. 1:25.)

* Bible references throughout are from the King James Bible.

If, then, any executive is sincerely searching for a code of ethics by which to operate his business at the most honorable level, he doesn't have to look far, no farther, in fact, than that little black book which is in every hotel room—and which ought to be on every executive's desk. And he must know that he cannot acquire its guidance by osmosis. He must first of all truly believe that the Bible is God talking to him and that it is his Christian duty to do what he is told. He must then read the Bible regularly, daily, seeking to understand it in context, and he should realize that though he may read it through many times he will never understand it all but he will nevertheless learn something new each time. He is sunk if he thinks he can be like the woman at the race track who baffled the bookies by picking the winner in every race. When they asked her how she did it, she said: "I close my eyes and stick a pin into the racing form, and the horse I hit is the horse I bet on." And when they asked her how she managed to pick the three-horse parlay, she said: "I used a fork." There is more to using the Bible properly than spot luck.

Furthermore, the proper use of the Bible involves more than familiarity with it, understanding, and even the acknowledgment of its truths. There must be commitment, commitment to the Lord, a surrender to the precepts of His book, the unreserved application of those precepts, the complete turning over to God of one's life—at home, on the road, at the club, in the office. The searching executive who decides for such a

9

commitment and is determined to live it shall be reborn and can take his first step into a new and vibrant world. Thereafter when he asks God's guidance in a business decision or God's help on a business project, he'd better be ready to move.

I know all this to be true from personal experience. There is no other explanation for what has happened to me.

I FOUND SOMETHING
BETTER THAN BASEBALL

I started out to be a ballplayer. Baseball was my first love and I never outgrew it. As a boy I frequently missed meals rather than miss a chance to play ball. Even now, regardless of the subject being discussed, I often find myself slipping into baseball jargon. Having thought of little else until I was almost a married man, I suppose it's natural that I should express myself best in terms of the game that was the driving force of my formative years. Perhaps at times the language has been out of place—when I've been teaching a Sunday School class, for example, or speaking from a pulpit or addressing a women's club. But maybe doing it my way assures me of a better chance of getting on base when I try to explain how I feel about the Lord, which is the driving force of my life now.

I suppose, too, it was my early love of sports that kept me from becoming much of a young scholar. I was born in Pocahontas, Arkansas, and started school there, and like Will Rogers I can say that I spent more time with McGuffy's Fourth Reader than McGuffy did. Like the boy whose favorite subject was recess, I lived for the moment when I could get out of class, collect a gang of kids and start a ballgame. I liked being catcher because this was where you could really do business, with never a dull moment. Because I was small and slight and kept up a torrent of chatter from behind the plate, people started calling me Pepper, which I preferred to my own name. Parents who decide to give their son a name like Marion had better teach him to defend himself before he is six years old because he is going to have a lot of trouble.

There was trouble in our home of another kind. My father, a tall, handsome, well-educated man, had been a partner in a dry-goods store that failed, and he seemed to fail with it. Fortunately, my mother was an excellent seamstress, and she supported the family by this means. I grew up among bolts of cloth that were bigger than I was; I remember the women who came to our house for fittings; I remember my mother sitting up late at night to finish her work. She was a small, attractive woman, austere and immaculate, quiet and patient. I was aware, of course, of the undercurrent of discontent in our home, but there was never any sign of it from my mother. I expect I was the closest to her of her four sons, probably because I was the youngest. Often at night I fell asleep on a couch near where she was working; I would be awakened when my father returned,

12

very late and very drunk, and I would watch helplessly as my mother tried to calm him and put him to bed. She was never argumentative with him, nor was she with my brothers and me. Whenever I went out to play, she would say: "Remember whose son you are." This admonition by itself was like a traffic light in my mind when I sensed myself verging on some boyish mischief. Many times I let myself lose a fight rather than risk tearing my shirt because I knew that repairing it would put an extra burden on an already overworked woman.

In 1905, when I was seven, we moved to McAlester, Oklahoma, where we hoped that my father would be able to get a fresh start for himself as a man and we would all get a fresh start as a family, but the situation remained unchanged. My mother was soon back at work as a dressmaker and my brothers and I found jobs in an effort to help out. I used to meet the 5:30 A.M. train from Oklahoma City and go through the cars selling newspapers while it was in the station. One morning I noticed that several departing passengers—and others just going to the station restaurant—had left current magazines behind, so I scooped them up and hurriedly sold them to other people. I thought this was very clever of me and when I got home I bragged to Mother about how I had earned some extra money.

"That's stealing," she said. "Those magazines didn't belong to you, and you had no right to sell them. I'm ashamed of you. Don't ever do anything like that again."

I didn't, although I realized I could easily have done

so on the sly. But my mother's approval was so important that getting tricky with her was unthinkable for all us boys, even when we were grown men. I still don't know what there was about her that made us all such devoted sons, except possibly that she was a genuine Christian and a devoted mother.

I was ten when I had my own experience with the American-boy tradition of running away from home. In my day, many boys tried this, even though most of them didn't stay away from home long enough to be missed. We probably got the idea from the Horatio Alger type books we read, about boys who ran away from unhappy homes or orphanages and then went on to become millionaires. It has been said that human beings are the only creatures who seek independence in their youth and dependence in their maturity, so I guess I was following the pattern. It came about this way:

One morning as the five-thirty was pulling out of McAlester, a beautiful pointer bird dog broke out of the baggage car and took off down the tracks. I caught him, claimed him, loved him on sight and, for reasons I have long since forgotten, called him Don. When I got him home, my mother noticed the words "Omaha, Nebraska" on his collar tag and she told me that before I could consider Don my dog I would have to place an ad in the Omaha papers to give the rightful owner a chance to claim him. With sinking heart, I sent the ad and money to Omaha, and for the next two weeks I gritted my teeth fearfully every time the mailman approached our house. But nothing came. Don was mine.

He was an excellent hunter. Men in town were soon talking about him and asking to rent him. In his own way, Don was contributing to the family larder. A haberdasher in town repeatedly offered to buy Don, but this, of course, was out of the question. One day, my father wanted to take Don hunting. Ordinarily this would have been all right with me, but on this particular day my father had started drinking early and I was afraid that he might lose the dog or even accidentally hurt him. So when my father commanded Don to accompany him out of the house, I told the dog to remain where he was.

Angry, my father gave me a brief but effective thumping, then took Don by the collar and led him away. They had gone about a block when I went outside and whistled to Don. He broke from my father and came running to me. Now angrier, my father raised his rifle and aimed at the dog as he ran. I was terrified that he might actually fire. Don reached me; I knelt and hugged him, my eyes on my father. In disgust, he lowered his rifle, turned and went on his way.

Convinced that neither Don nor I would be safe any longer, I decided that we both ought to be on our own but separate ways. I took Don to the haberdasher and sold him for $25, then I went to a pal of mine, a one-armed boy called "Wingy" Dill, and asked him if he would be interested in running away from home with me. He was. We decided to go to Fort Smith, Arkansas, where my oldest brother, Maurice, was working as a printer, and we agreed that it would be smart for us to find jobs before we let Maurice know we were in town so that we could thereby prove to him that we could take care of ourselves. Wingy announced that he would seek a job as an electrician's helper and I planned on starting my life as a man of the world in the position of Western Union messenger boy. Our minds made up, we went to the McAlester railroad station and bought two tickets to Fort Smith out of the money I had been paid for Don.

We arrived at Fort Smith in the late afternoon. The long train ride had taken much of the spunk out of us, and we were two scared kids as we stood there, unnoticed and ignored, in the railroad station. I'm sure that if either of us had even hinted at heading back home both of us would have been on the next train. But then the excitement of finding ourselves on our own in what struck us as a bustling big city began to seep in and some of our daring returned.

"What do we do now?" Wingy asked.

"We'd better find jobs," I said. "I'm going over to the Western Union office."

"Okay. I'll hunt up an electrician who needs a helper."

"Okay. Let's meet back here in an hour," I said, and we parted.

I found the Western Union office easily, and when I asked the manager for a job he said I could have one if

I had a bicycle. "I'll be back with a bicycle tomorrow," I said, and I walked out of the store and bumped smack into my brother.

He was dumbfounded. He gripped me by the shoulders and demanded: "What are you doing here?"

I was both staggered and relieved to see Maurice, but from the expression on his face I also knew I was in trouble. I told him what had happened at home, that Wingy and I had run away and that I had sold the dog to raise the fare. I also explained that I had just got a job and that I expected Wingy would have one soon.

He said: "You crazy kid, you're going home. Don't you know Mother must be worried sick about you?"

"I was going to write her," I offered.

Maurice asked: "Do you have any of the money left?" When I said yes, he said: "Then let me handle it for you." I gave it to him, and he said: "I'll wire Mother now and tell her you'll be home tomorrow. She must be terribly worried."

When Wingy saw Maurice and me together, he got that glum look that kids wear when they realize the jig is up, but I half suspected that he was glad about it. He hadn't found a job, and the fun of being on his own in a strange town had worn off; he was more than ready to go home. When I told him that Maurice had wired my mother and that she would tell his, he nodded, then rolled his eyes in expectation of the stormy reception he knew he would get from his father. The same thought sent shudders through me. As a sampler, Maurice was stern with both of us for the rest of the evening. We slept in his room. Downstairs neighbors were playing a music box full blast, which kept me awake, and as I lay there I started thinking of the magnitude of what I had done and what awaited me. I began to cry and couldn't stop and I didn't get any sleep all night. I was a sorry and miserable little rebel.

It was dusk the next evening when Wingy and I stepped from the train back at McAlester, both of us torn between the urge to rush to our homes and the dread of facing the music. Wingy asked: "Are you gonna be on time for supper at your house?"

"No, I don't think so," I said.

"Me, neither. Let's get a hamburger."

So we spent the last of our riches on hamburgers, nibbling at them absently, like doomed men at their last meal, until we could stall no longer. Then we said goodbye dismally and Wingy went his way and I went mine. As I turned into Apache Street, I started to whistle; I was always whistling, but this time the tune had a mournful sound. When I reached the gate of our house, I froze.

I could see my father in the living room, reading a newspaper. He had evidently heard me. He lowered his paper and looked out the window for a few moments, then he got up and went to the door. We stood there looking at each other for what seemed forever, and then he gruffly ordered: "Come in here."

My first impulse was to run away again, but then my

mother came to the door. I remember she was wearing a gingham apron and she had her hands deep in the pockets. She said: "Honey, come in."

I went in, giving my father a wide berth as I passed him. Mother asked: "Are you hungry?"

"I just had a hamburger," I said.

"Wash up, and I'll fix you something," she said.

While I was washing up in the kitchen, I could hear my father's angry rumble over the soft but insistent voice of my mother. At last, my mother came into the kitchen alone, and as she was passing me on her way to the stove she paused and put a hand on my shoulder and looked at me. The remnants of worry and hurt I saw in her eyes cut me deeper than any punishment my father might have given me, and I vowed there and then that I would never again knowingly do anything that would distress her. And since I knew that the entire episode had been the outgrowth of my father's drinking, I made up my mind that I would forever avoid the habit that could bring so much misery into a home.

A short time later, my mother decided to leave my father. My two older brothers were already away from home; Stanley, the third son, was to go to Jonesboro, Arkansas, to be apprenticed to an uncle as a plumber's helper, and Mother and I were to live with her brother in Oak Park, Illinois. My father went to the train with us and helped us get settled in our places. I remember that I was sitting next to my mother, and so I heard my father when he leaned over and said gruffly to her: "Sally, you'll be back."

"No, Sam, I'll never be back," my mother said, and that was the end of it. She never went back.

There had been a blizzard in Chicago and the snow was piled high on the streets on the cold, windy night we walked out of the LaSalle Street Station. I sensed for the first time the tensions and tempo of a big city. My mother had been in Chicago before and, knowing her way around, led me up the stairs to the elevated railroad platform where we boarded the Lake Street train for Oak Park. There were open platforms at the ends of the cars, and my mother permitted me to stand out there for the long ride to the suburb. I was overwhelmed by the endlessness of the city: mile after mile the lighted houses stretched away as far as I could see, like a carpet of stars.

My Uncle George lived in a big frame house that still stands. He and Aunt Florence and their five children occupied the first two floors; my mother's parents lived on the third floor, and we moved in with them. I was now in a home where the men not only earned the money but also made the decisions and disciplined the children constructively as well as punitively—all of which was a new experience for me. Previously, when my father gave me an order I usually looked to my mother for an approving nod before carrying it out, presumably because I realized that it was she who had my best interests at heart. Now that changed. Both

Grandfather and Uncle George were devout Christians whose attitudes toward family matters were rooted in love, but tempered with the understanding that everybody knew who the boss was. It wasn't necessary for anybody to second any of their decisions or instructions. One evening, soon after our arrival, I didn't like something that had been served for dinner and I left it on my plate. Grandfather noticed and said that I shouldn't waste the food which the Lord had provided. I said something sassy, probably to the effect that the Lord could have it back, and for the rest of the meal Grandfather ignored me icily. Later, Mother took me aside, pointed out that I had been rude and ungrateful, and made me go to Grandfather and apologize. From this I caught on pretty quick, and as soon as I did I became quite happy in my new home.

The Bible was an important factor on all floors of our house. There were prayers at meals, led either by Grandfather or Uncle George, and then Grandfather read the Bible aloud every night. Uncle George was an officer of the church and taught Sunday School at a Presbyterian church in Chicago, to which we all traveled by streetcar every Sunday. On summer evenings we would all gather on the porch and usually end the day with a family songfest comprised mostly of hymns. Family conversations frequently touched on religious matters, if only to thank God for something good that had happened or to ask Him to help us or our neighbors with some problem.

Little of all this rubbed off on me, for the same reason, I suppose, that little of my schooling did. The reason was baseball. I was obsessed by the game. Although I couldn't memorize the Bible verses that had been assigned at last week's Sunday School class, I could rattle off a play-by-play description of any Cub game you cared to mention, and although I never mastered the multiplication tables I could calculate what each player's hit was doing to his batting average while the ball was still in the air.

In school, my mind was on the ballgame which had been started before class and would be resumed at morning recess, during lunch time, at afternoon recess and after school, each time picking up exactly where we left off. In church, my mind was on the fact that my roller skates were in the bushes outside and that as soon as I could get out of the place I'd skate down to Cubs Park, then at Polk and Harrison Streets, hide my skates in a tree, then shinny over the tin fence and make my way to the Cubs' side. If you caught a foul ball and returned it, you got a free pass to another game. Like other kids who loved the Cubs, I hated surrendering the ball when it was hit by one of my heroes—even at the cost of the free pass. But you had to be fast on your feet to keep the ball: economy-minded Charles Murphy, then the Cubs' owner, would chase a kid all the way to Cheyenne to get the ball back.

Despite the distraction that baseball was, I nevertheless learned many things from it which I subsequently was able to apply effectively to every area of life. I learned, for example, that playing as a dedicated member of a team was the only way to become important to the team. Naturally, I wanted to be the best catcher in the world, but I discovered that no matter how dazzling I might be behind the plate, I wasn't of much value to the team unless I kept in mind the problems of the men covering the bases while there was a runner on. Also, every player is concerned about his hitting average; but when the situation calls for a sacrifice bunt to advance the man on first, even the best batter has got to try for it for the good of the team. In building a business, a family or a church, we've got to think about the other fellow's problems, help him do his job and even make personal sacrifices if the job is to be done at all. This sense of responsibility toward others, whatever the effort, results in a team spirit which though it can't guarantee a pennant at least provides more of a chance for one. As yet, nobody has pitched a 27-strikeouts game, but hundreds of no-hitters have been made possible by the capable and concerned men who were backing up the pitcher, and everybody on the team knew it and developed into a better player individually because of it.

Another lesson I've learned from baseball is to take care of a problem when it arises, before it gets out of control, a lesson derived from the ballgame in which a powerful left-handed batter sent a sizzling line drive straight at the head of the first-baseman who decided to duck rather than risk decapitation. The rightfielder, racing in, misjudged the ball, and it shot past him and hit the fence. On a play like this, the second-baseman moves into right field for the relay, while the pitcher and shortstop move in to cover second. By the time this second-baseman got the ball and spun around, the runner was on his way to third. Surprised, the secondbagger sent a wild throw to third that hit the players' bench. When the ball bounced back, the third base coach picked it up and threw it into the water bucket, and the runner kept going and scored. The umpire came roaring up to the coach, shouting: "You're out of the game! Why on earth did you do a thing like that?" The coach said: "Well, it was too hot for anybody to handle." Sudden problems, whether in business, the home or in church, sometimes seem too hot to handle, but I've observed that when I duck the issue anything that happens afterward only makes matters worse. Usually I've ducked when the problem involved some unpleasantness, perhaps correcting a man who worked for me or exercising my paternal duties at home or when confronted with a personality conflict with a fellow member of a church board, and I've always regretted it. Scripture says: "A kind word turneth away wrath." Whatever the situation, the kind word I've used is the story about that line drive, to explain why I'm not going to duck a problem or the other fellow shouldn't have.

One problem I had in my youth I couldn't do anything about—my size. I was too small to play ball with the big fellows who were much better at it than boys of my build. This agonized me for years. After I finished grammar school in 1912, I got a job as office boy at a wholesale paper company on Dearborn Street at the Chicago River, and evenings I took a course in business arithmetic at the YMCA, but none of this sidetracked me. My heart was still set on becoming a ballplayer and I just couldn't get interested in anything else. During the noon hour, a group of muscle-bound teamsters used to play ball in the parking lot behind our office building, in the area now occupied by the famous Marina Towers. At first I begged those fellows every day to let me get in the game, and they always said no because, though I was then fourteen, they thought I was eight and definitely not in their league. After a while I gave up asking and just watched from an office window as I ate my lunch. One day when they were short a man they saw me at the window and told me to come down and play. When I got up to bat I walloped that first pitch right over the warehouse and into the river. From then on when they chose sides I was in great demand, and I suppose I felt like David must have felt after he took care of Goliath —on my way to becoming king.

Some of these men played on the semiprofessional teams that were so popular in Chicago at the time. Several of the teams were so well established that they organized themselves into a league, but for the most part the teams were made up of men who either worked together or lived in the same neighborhood, who liked playing ball together and who found more interest in the game when they put a couple of dollars into it. The men at work began asking me to play on their semipro teams and I was more than happy to. In addition to enjoying the game, the extra money came in handy, since my job paid me only five dollars a week.

The games were played on Sundays, which displeased my mother not only because it was the Lord's day but particularly because of the money involved. She was convinced that I was gambling. I carefully explained to her that baseball was a matter of skill, not luck or guesswork, that the experience was preparing me for the day when I hoped to play baseball as a career, and also that we needed the money. Uncle George had died about a year after we moved to Oak Park, and we all had to give up the big house. Mother, her parents, and my brother Stanley and I had moved into a smaller house on St. Louis Avenue in Chicago, on the West Side near Garfield Park. My grandparents were too old to work; most of our household finances were met by my mother's older brother, Morgan, but the rest of us brought in what we could; Mother by resuming her sewing and Stanley and I by our jobs. However, Mother's decision to let me continue playing ball was not based on money. She knew I'd be miserable if I had to stop. The only condition she stipulated was that I attend Sunday School at the Walnut Avenue Methodist Church before hotfooting it over to the ballpark. To this I readily agreed, although I had to exercise the utmost restraint to hang around until the choir finished the last Amen.

In 1914, I played ball more and more with a bunch of fellows nearer my own age who loved the game as much as I did. We were pretty good, so we agreed to form our own semipro team for the next season. The Boston Braves had won the 1914 World Series in four straight games. Hopefully, we called ourselves the Chicago Braves. All winter we talked baseball and when spring came, we went to work. Baseball was played differently in those days. The emphasis was less on home runs, more on infield action. Ballparks were laid out in such a way that only real muscle-men could hit homers, and if a man hit eight or ten of them in a season he was considered a real homerun king. Scores were therefore much tighter; a team could feel safe with a one- or two-run lead. These days, the fans want more action. Parks are designed so that even the lightest man can put one over the fence occasionally, and the heavy hitters are expected to come up with eight or ten homers in a couple of weeks. Pitching, too, has changed. In my day, teams didn't carry the stables of relief pitchers that they do today. One man pitched the whole game. And if he got into trouble, everybody else on the team had to work harder to get him out of it.

When in 1915 the Chicago Braves started spring training (I think it was on New Year's Day), we concentrated on bunting, running bases and sliding, all of which we knew we'd have to master if we hoped to be able to pick up a run when we needed it. Near the big empty lot where we practiced was a boulevard that had a grass-covered road divider running down it, with trees about fifty feet apart. To practice sliding, we'd go over there and line up at one end of the block. Then each of us would take off at top speed, one kid after the other, sliding into tree after tree, hooking the tree either with a left foot or a right while throwing the body away from the tree. The idea was to get the corner of the base while offering a poor target to the fellow trying to tag you. Ty Cobb was famous for this, and since he was our hero it was natural that we should want to imitate him. Day after day of practice greatly improved our sliding technique. It must also have given heart attacks to a lot of drivers who suddenly found themselves approaching a bunch of kids who looked as if they were all about to slide out into the middle of the street.

We worked as hard on our bunting. Ordinarily, if a team could get a runner on base, particularly with nobody out, a bunt was automatically called in order to advance the man to second. But we felt we could improve on this, and so we practiced every day with a definite purpose in mind: to train each man to bunt the ball far enough away from the catcher and pitcher to make the third-baseman come in to field it. The man on first had orders to run with the pitch, gambling on the hope that the bunt would be good, and instead of stopping at second, he would go on to third. Most of the time nobody was there to cover the base. We pulled this play a great many times during the season and it won a lot of ballgames for us.

In order to buy uniforms we raffled off a five-dollar gold piece and sold enough tickets to raise several hundred dollars. We then proceeded to a sporting-goods store where we were measured for real Big League uniforms. Ours had an Indian head on the shirt and the word "Braves" across the chest. As I remember, some of the boys feathered their nests with a few gloves and balls while the rest of us were being measured.

When the 1915 season opened, we had a real eager-beaver ball club. We played our first game on our own lot, against a team representing a real estate company. It was the custom at these games to pass the hat among the spectators, but to add some personal interest the teams also made side bets, winner take all, and the size of the bet depended on how much a team could raise from its players. At this game, the side bet was seven dollars—and the Braves won it. The side bets gave me, as catcher, an extra job. The umpire always held the money. Once in a while a fight broke out during a game, sometimes involving everybody on both teams, and it wasn't uncommon for the umpire to use that as an opportunity to take off with the stakes. It was my job to see that this didn't happen.

That first victory was the start of a stretch that went through about thirty ballgames without a loss, each game tougher than the last as our good record brought us up against better teams. Though we weren't in the Chicago Semi-pro League and had no regular schedule, we were a popular team and could always find another club willing to take us on. One indication of how we rated was that we were one of the few semipro teams in the city whose box scores were published regularly in the Chicago newspapers. Also, we had a fine following and sometimes the customary collections ran over a hundred dollars. Between this and the side bets, we had a good year financially, and yet this didn't mean as much to most of us as the fact that we knew we had one of the best teams in town. Encouraged, we decided to close the season by challenging the Chicago Giants, a League team with an outstanding record.

We played these fellows on November 17, at Albany and Lake Streets, behind a canvas fence. Expecting a big crowd, we rented a bleacher section. It was a cold day, got dark early, and we had a few snow flurries, as I recall. I also recall that the Braves weren't doing so well. When we came to bat at the end of the fifth we were losing 1-0. Desperate, we decided we had to do something about it. Since we couldn't see the ball well enough to hit it, we decided to let it hit us—to take a pitch, as we called it.

As it happened, I was the first man up and I knew I had to get on base, which I promptly did by getting hit by the first pitch. The next two men up followed suit, and in short order the pond was filled with ducks; three on and nobody out. The Giants appealed to the umpire but to no avail, and it was a sure bet that the next man up would get hit even if he had to take it between the eyes. However, fate intervened. As I was taking a lead off third base, ready to score on anything, I heard a crash behind me. I turned around and saw that the bleachers had collapsed, and the next thing I knew everybody was out on the field. That ended the ballgame and we lost it, 1-0. Fortunately, nobody was hurt, but it was a dismal finish for our season and we shed real tears over it.

Those tears showed how we felt about baseball. We played to win, always. That's why we practiced so hard. That's why we were ready to risk our skulls to get on base. As long as we all continued to feel this way we had a team spirit that made us unbeatable, notwithstanding that last game. When we got over the shock of that game, we all grew impatient with winter and itched for the next season to arrive. But something happened to some of the fellows during the intervening months. As might be expected, offers came from other teams, teams not as good as ours but teams with more money, and a few of the men found the offers irresistible. I could understand this up to a point. After all, everybody wants to get ahead, and to some people this means earning more money. But what infuriated me at the time was that any of us would be willing to play with any other team but the terrific club we had put together, no matter how much was in it. To me, this was treason.

It was also my first experience with a human failing I

31

subsequently encountered many times in many people and in many circumstances: the failing of creeping indifference. This is bound to strike a person whose heart is not entirely involved in a specific matter, whether it is baseball or business or, as I discovered later, the Bible. In fact, it wasn't until I got over my own creeping indifference toward the Bible that I became aware of how many times this human failing provided a turning point in my life, either when it struck me or those with whom I was associated. You can tell that the indifference has started creeping when you experience a change in your motivation from outgoing to incoming. The Chicago Braves, for example, fell apart when some of the fellows cared less about the team and its victories and more about how much they could earn playing baseball. Anybody who runs a business knows what can happen to the company when any members of his team undergo this kind of reversal toward the product or the service. Significantly, the Bible stresses this point of outgoing wholeheartedness repeatedly. We are instructed, for instance, to love the Lord, our God, with all of our heart, with all of our soul, with all our might. Clearly, then, there is no room for halfhearted indifference in this area. Moreover, Paul wrote to the Colossians that everything they did in their daily life should be done as though they were doing it for the Lord, not merely for men. To me, this can only mean that we must always do our best and give our all. And the Book of Revelation is even more specific on how God feels about indifference, when He indicts the people at Laodicea with: "I know thy works, that thou art neither cold nor hot: I would thou wert cold or hot. So then because thou art lukewarm, and neither cold nor hot, I will spue thee out of my mouth." (Rev. 3:15, 16.)

Looking back, I realize I was too young at the time to view the creeping indifference of some members of the Braves as anything but the worst kind of disloyalty. I was bitter about it for a while but, naturally, this passed, and today I remember the Braves with affection because of the tremendous spirit we did have during that 1915 season. In later years, when I found myself working with men who had the same spirit toward what we were doing, I'd always be reminded of my old team. Over the years, I have watched this spirit seep out of some of the men, just as it seeped out of some of my teammates, and with the years I have come to understand why this happens. But before I could acquire this understanding, I had to undergo the experience which made the understanding possible. It was the experience that changed my life.

It happened in 1930. I was married, had two children, and, in the first months of the Depression, was struggling to put a business on its feet. My mother was getting along in years, so as a filial gesture I accompanied her to church on Sunday nights. Dr. Harry Ironside was the pastor of Moody Church and Mother loved to hear him. I enjoyed being with her, but I had so many problems on my mind that I didn't get much out of the sermons myself. The business I had started was a moth-proofing service; with the Depression on, few people had enough money to buy anything that moths might eat. So I was worried about how my own family was going to eat.

Sitting there next to Mother in Moody Church one Sunday evening, I was brooding about where to turn for work. I was scarcely aware of Pastor Ironside's voice, let alone his words. But worrying about yourself can be an exhausting experience, and so it was mostly out of fatigue that my attention gradually drifted from my problems to the pulpit.

Dr. Ironside was talking about the Bible, sternly criticizing the people who ignored it. As I listened, I developed the disturbing feeling that he was preaching right at me and nobody else. I had, I realized, neglected the Bible. We had a Bible at home. My mother read it regularly, but I rarely looked at it, and not since my boyhood days in Sunday School had I given it any serious attention. Sitting there, I knew in my heart that I was one of the people Dr. Ironside was talking about.

He then began to stress the Divine authority of the Bible, explaining that as the Word of God it was the Rule of God, the rules for our lives, recorded by men who were inspired by Him as they wrote, and that as such every Christian was obligated to follow these rules. Up to this point of my life, I had never given the Bible a thought as the God-written authority over me. But now that I did think about it I recognized that this

34

must be true. Scant as was my knowledge of the Bible, my adverse experiences in dealing with men assured me that mere men could not have written the Bible because mere men were incapable of the selfless and noble ideas in it. Unquestionably, God had to be its source. I squirmed as I became more aware of my neglect of God's Word.

As he concluded his message, Dr. Ironside pleaded with the congregation to love the Bible more, to read it more often, to follow it more closely. Then he asked those who were ready to make these commitments, to repent of their sins and accept Christ as their personal Saviour, to come to the altar as a public acknowledgment before God of their decision. I had never responded to an altar call in my life. The idea alone made me uncomfortable, and I'm sure that if I had ever had the urge to respond I would have squelched it rather than make a spectacle of myself. But this time it was different. I believed fully that everything Dr. Ironside had said about the Bible was absolutely true; I realized that his accusations of neglect applied to me; I recognized that I had to do something about it. Mother, who always seemed able to read my mind, looked at me and asked: "Marion, don't you want to go?" I said I did. Without second thought, without hesitation, without embarrassment, I arose and went forward. I was doing what I felt I had to do, the only sensible thing I could do. I had been asked to acknowledge a decision, so I did.

35

At the altar, a man holding a Bible read to me from the Gospel of John: "He [Jesus] came unto his own, and his own received him not. But as many as received him, to them gave he power to become sons of God, *even* to them that believe on his name: Which were born, not of blood, nor of the will of the flesh, nor of the will of man, but of God." (St. John 1:11, 12.)

As I listened, I asked God to forgive the sins of my life. I gave my heart and my life to Christ, and, according to God's Word, I was reborn that moment. I became a son of God. I became a Christian.

I don't know what I expected to happen. I don't recall any tremendous amount of emotion at the moment, and yet there was a realization in my heart that something was going on. I was like the man who having seen the flash of lightning in a storm was waiting expectantly for the thunder. A cataclysmic change had occurred in me, I knew that. But I had no idea what to do about it.

Moments later, Mother's eyes were full of tears as she said: "I'm glad you did that, Marion."

"So am I," I admitted. It was surely the answer to her many prayers over many years, prayers which I was going to need for many years to come.

Under Dr. Ironside's exhortation and Mother's encouragement, I began to read my Bible. Because of my lack of experience with the Bible, there were times when I felt I was reading it in a foreign language. But I kept at it. When I discovered that Paul, that great servant of the Lord, had to spend thirteen years learning the faith before he felt qualified to go out and do the Lord's work, I figured there might be some hope for me, and so I struggled on. Meanwhile, I tried to move more in what I considered the circle of the Lord. Eventually I conducted Bible classes for a group of boys, and I coached the church's baseball team. At home, daily Bible reading and discussion were becoming a family custom.

And I kept waiting for the thunder. I had yet to realize that the thunder was supposed to come from me, not the Lord. Ahead of me was the discovery that until I gave myself to the Lord as wholeheartedly as I did to baseball and my business, I couldn't expect to be much aware of His real presence in my life. After I made both the discovery and the commitment, I was able to look back over my life and perceive that this was exactly what the Lord had been wanting me to do all along.

✻ ✻ ✻ 3 ✻ ✻ ✻

SERVICE IS A BANNER

God guides us. Repeatedly the Bible assures us that He will, provided we do our part. In the Book of Proverbs we are told: "Trust in the Lord with all thine heart; and lean not unto thine own understanding. In all thy ways acknowledge him, and he shall direct thy paths." (Prov. 3: 5, 6.) I can't think of a better way for a businessman to avoid ulcers than to conduct his affairs according to this Bible promise. There is nothing materialistic about this. It is simply a matter of taking the Lord at His Word. Proverbs goes on to say: "Honor the Lord with thy substance, and with the first fruits of all thine increase: So shall thy barns be filled with plenty, and thy presses shall burst out with the new wine." To me, this is a clear indication that the Lord is interested in my "substance"—my business—and the way I operate it, and if I run it in a way that honors the Lord I won't have too much to worry about.

Time and again, businessmen have said to me: "I just

can't bring the Lord into my business." The only answer to that is: "Then, mister, you'd better get out of your business." Presumably, the man who says he can't bring the Lord into his business has given the matter some thought. I have often found that the reason a man feels this way is that he doesn't know much about the Lord in the first place. When possible, I've pursued the subject, asking: "What is there in the Bible that you feel you can't possibly apply in your business?" The most frequent answer: "The Sermon on the Mount." Each time I hear this I realize the truth in the saying that a little knowledge can be dangerous.

Over the years, I have read and heard more about the Sermon on the Mount than any other part of the Bible. As beautiful as the Sermon is and as perfect as its precepts are for a Christian world, it can only be understood when placed in its proper time. Because some men feel they can't live up to the Sermon, they decide the Bible has nothing else for them, and so they ignore it completely. I've been asked: "When I find out someone has infringed on my patents, do I turn the other cheek?" And: "Am I supposed to love the competitor who is dirty-dealing me into bankruptcy?" According to the Sermon on the Mount, the answer is yes; but according to other portions of the Bible, the answer is: "Use the brains God gave you for the time in which you live."

John 18:21-23, for example, tells of the time when Jesus didn't turn the other cheek. He had been arrested

and was being cross-examined by the high priests about
His doctrine, and He answered:

> Why askest thou me? ask them which heard me, what I
> have said unto them: behold, they know what I said.
> And when he had thus spoken, one of the officers which
> stood by struck Jesus with the palm of his hand, saying,
> Answerest thou the high priest so?
> Jesus answered him, If I have spoken evil, bear witness
> of the evil: but if well, why smitest thou me?

Moreover, Matthew, Mark and Luke write of Jesus's
anger when He discovered that merchants and money
changers had turned the temple into a supermarket—He
threw them out. It would appear, then, that even the
Saviour felt there were times when He had to hold His
ground or get other people off His grounds.

God doesn't expect us to act like fools or to neglect
our proper duties to others for His sake. Loving us, He
wants only the best for us and is always ready to show
us the way. Loving Him, we honor Him by conducting
our affairs His way, which is the Bible's way. To be able
to do this, we have to know what is in the Bible—the
whole Bible, not just a few pages of it. I have yet to hear
a truly Christian businessman say that the Bible gives
him any trouble in his office. On the other hand, the
executive who says he can't bring the Bible into his business, usually because of the mandates of the Sermon on
the Mount, seems either to be showing his ignorance or
dodging the issue.

The seventy-third Psalm demonstrates this dramatically. Addressing the Lord, the Psalmist starts out by admitting that for a while he had been envious of "the prosperity of the wicked." Here was this fellow, a child of the Lord, struggling to get along and seemingly not making much headway, and he looked around and saw that corrupt and evil men were piling up profits, power and pleasures. Not surprisingly, he considered changing his ways in order to get some of the gravy, but then he says: "Until I went into the sanctuary of God, then understood I their end. Surely thou didst set them in slippery places: thou castedst them down into destruction. How are they *brought* down into desolation, as in a moment! They are utterly consumed with terrors." He then apologizes to the Lord for having thought for a moment of turning away from Him, and he says: "So foolish *was* I, and ignorant: I was *as* a beast before thee. Nevertheless I *am* continually with thee: thou has holden *me* by my right hand. Thou shalt guide me with thy counsel, and afterward receive me *to* glory."

I interpret this as meaning that if, during my lifetime, I commit my way to God, He will direct me with His counsel and when my end comes He will take me into His Home. This much I know: I won't get better counsel anywhere else. And this is my confidence: As long as the Lord is first in every area of my life, I'm not going to worry too much about the gravy. It will come along, one way or another. The idea is well put in this little verse:

Here's a thought for today that I bring you,
Without preaching or sermon or text:
If you're getting ahead in this world, just be sure
You're not getting behind in the next.

The businessman who realizes he's not getting ahead much in this world will do something about it fast. He will call in the experts to help him solve his problems. The same practical procedure applies to making headway in the next world, only in this case the expertise is a man's thorough, personal, practical understanding and application of the Bible's teachings. For me, however, the Bible provides the best source of guidance for getting ahead in both worlds. In fact, I can't see how anybody can separate the two. As a Christian, I am involved in the spiritual world in the same way that, as a human being, I am involved in the world around me, and my Bible is the link between the two.

I therefore regard my Bible as a cross, the vertical bar representing my relationship with God and the horizontal bar representing my relationship with my fellow man. In the vertical relationship, I acknowledge God by loving Him, by obeying Him, by serving Him, by depending on Him, and He acknowledges me through His love, guidance and blessings. God must also be involved in my relationships with the world around me—the horizontal relationship—or I run the risk of merely paying Him lip service. "Not everybody who cries 'Lord! Lord!' will be saved," the Bible warns, pointing out the risks of mere lip service. In my daily life, then, I acknowledge

God by the way I conduct my daily affairs. The Lord
has been clear about what that conduct should be. In
Mark's tenth chapter we can read about how upset
James and John became when Jesus could not promise
them a seat on either side of Him when He returned
to His Kingdom. The other Apostles were angry at
James and John for even asking but, as Mark writes:
(10:42-44)

> "Jesus called them to him and saith unto them, Ye know
> that they which are accounted to rule over the Gentiles ex-
> ercise lordship over them; and their great ones exercise au-
> thority upon them.
> But so shall it not be among you: but whosoever will be
> great among you shall be your minister.
> And whosoever of you will be the chiefest shall be servant
> of all.
> For even the Son of man came not to be ministered unto
> but to minister and to give his life as a ransom for many."

Other Bible passages contain similar indications that
Jesus Christ, the Son of God, looked upon Himself as
a servant. In recounting the same episode, Luke quotes
the Master as saying: "I am among you as he that
serveth." We know that after the Last Supper Jesus
washed the Apostles' feet, a job that was ordinarily done
by the lowest servant in the household when the sandal-
wearing guests came in off the dusty roads. Apparently
the Apostles got the point. James, writing to the persecuted and scattered first Christians, begins with: "James,
the servant of God and of our Lord Jesus Christ, to the
twelve tribes that are in the dispersion: a greeting."

Peter and Jude likewise identified themselves as servants, and Paul wrote the Corinthians: "Though I be free from all men, yet have I made myself servant unto all."

For the man, then, who is seeking guidance on how to run a business based on Christian ethics and principles, there it is. We must become servants, servants first of all of the Lord and then, in His Name, servants unto all. We must serve. We must give service. Serving the Lord, we must give Him the only things He wants of us: our love and obedience. And we bear witness to this love and obedience by the type of service we give others. In business, the others are our stockholders, our boards, our staffs, our fellow businessmen, our competition and, most of all, our customers. It must be a full-throttle effort or the deal is off, for once we begin fudging on our service to others we're ineluctably fudging on our service to God—and God we cannot deceive. So if we want to be Christian businessmen, if we ever hope to be able to recognize the guidance with which God has filled the Bible, we must decide here and now that we are going to be good and faithful servants and, like Paul, ask Him: "Master, what would you have me do?" The answer will come in terms of what we must do for others, toward others and with others, and the answers are all in the Bible. Thus the cross of the vertical and horizontal aspects of the Bible become the Cross of Christianity which we should carry not as a burden but as a banner.

It took me a long time to learn this, but then I had a lot of other things to learn along the way. For one thing,

I had to learn that religion meant different things to different people. My first experience with this occurred when I was a youngster, and perhaps it is one of the reasons religion didn't mean much to me for a long time. The 1916 season for the Chicago Braves was a severe disappointment for me. Because several of the fellows had gone to other teams for more money, we had some new personnel on the team, players who lacked both the ability and the spirit of our original club. It just wasn't the same. I decided it was time for me to do something about getting my own baseball career on the move.

One of the Chicago newspapers sponsored an annual contest to find outstanding young players in the city. You entered the contest by filling out a coupon published in the paper and you were subsequently notified when to appear at Cubs Park or Sox Park for the tryouts. Several hundred boys applied and by the process of elimination, twenty-five boys were chosen for the finals. There were three prizes: a roadtrip with the Cubs, a roadtrip with the Sox and a bench-seat with the president of the American League at the World Series. Also, Big League scouts watched the contest for any promising players, so there was a lot riding on it. The winners were selected during a play-off game at Cubs Park by three judges, men prominent in business or politics, sometimes both.

I entered the 1916 contest and made it to the play-off. As all the finalists were changing clothes for the game, I noticed that one of the fellows was wearing a scapular, the cloth religious article that Catholics wear around the neck. I knew this kid. He had been on the Braves for a while and also we had gone to the same Sunday school together, so I knew he wasn't a Catholic any more than I was. When I asked him why he had it on, he just shook his head and grinned.

The play-off went okay for me. I put my whole heart into the game, not only because I wanted to win a trip but because that was the way I felt about baseball. I must have made a good showing because I was among the seven or eight, including the kid with the scapular, who were called aside, had our pictures taken and were told that the winners would be chosen from our group. The announcement was to appear in the next day's paper, with the first edition coming out late that same evening.

That evening I got a telephone call from the paper's sports editor, asking me to come down to the office. He wouldn't tell me on the phone what was up, so, tense and worried, I made the trip downtown. He had bad news. In the course of their deliberations, the judges had cut the competition down to four players, two of them so outstanding that there was no question about their victory. The remaining choice was between me and another lad. When he couldn't hold his edition any longer, the editor had called the judges for a decision. They said they had just agreed on the other boy. Surprised, the editor asked the basis for the decision, and the judge said: "He's a Catholic." Then the editor said to me that there had been rumors that for political reasons this was going to be a good year for the Catholics. This was news to me, though evidently my friend with the scapular had heard about it. I was, of course, very disappointed.

"Never mind, Pepper," the editor said. "Next year, all you'll have to do is enter the contest, and I can promise you right now that you'll get a trip."

I didn't want that. If I couldn't get a trip on my ability, I didn't want one as a consolation prize. Fortunately, I was young enough not to become permanently embittered by the experience. I had nothing against the other boy; after all, he didn't make the decision. Moreover, most of the Braves were Catholics; I liked them and we got along fine. Even so, losing out because of my religion left me hurt and puzzled, and I remember thinking: "Well, if this is what religion is all about, you can have it."

As it turned out, there was no "next year." In the summer of 1917, America was at war. The newspaper cancelled the annual contest, never held another, and so I never got another chance to win a trip on my own. It was during that summer I met the girl I eventually married. I first saw Lillian while she was trying to play tennis in Garfield Park. I was a pretty good tennis player, and it pained me to watch somebody having such a bad time with the game. For this reason, I went over to give her a few tips. After we talked for a few minutes I realized how pretty she was, and after a few tennis lessons we began to date. In those days, young people did not go out on dates as frequently as they do now. You courted a girl by visiting her at home, where her watchful parents could keep things under control. Often after Lil's father escorted me to the front door, I would run around to the back of the house and shinny up the rain pipe to the second-floor porch, and we would sit there and listen to the orchestra playing in the beer garden below. Lil's father had a hacking cough which was, I think, certainly to my best interest. We could hear him approaching when he came into the kitchen for anything, and this gave me time to shinny down the rain pipe and be on my way. Then when her father would ask: "Lil, are you alone?" she could say yes.

In June 1918, I was on the porch with Lil when my mother telephoned with the heartbreaking news that my brother Burette, who had joined the Army, had been killed in France. As soon as I could, I went down to the Marines recruiting office to enlist. It was a crushing blow to me to be rejected because I was underweight, and the recruiting sergeant must have sensed my disappointment because he said: "Listen, kid, go on out and eat a lot of bananas and drink a lot of water and then come back here and try again." For a couple of hours I stuffed myself with so many bananas that even now I can't stand the sight of one, but when I went back I made the weight. I was told I would be notified when to report for duty. I was sworn in on Armistice Day.

Apparently nobody told the Marines that the war was

over. At Parris Island I was put through a grueling combat training that quickly took off my banana poundage, plus much more weight I couldn't spare. Also, when it was discovered that I had played semipro ball I was assigned to coach the camp team. So whenever the non-players in my outfit got a few minutes to recuperate on their sacks, I was out in the hot sun trying to put a team together. The worst thing a Marine can do is admit that he's pooped, so I didn't admit it. But I figured it wouldn't be long before I'd end up a stretcher case.

Unknown to me, my mother had appealed to the Red Cross to get me a dependency discharge. The first I heard about it was when the company commander called me in and asked: "Private Wade, would you like to get out of the Marine Corps?"

"Would I?!" I said. "I can be packed and at the railroad station before you can sign the papers."

That was the end of me and the Marines. Back in Chicago, I returned to work for the paper company on Dearborn Street, this time as a salesman on commission. I was then twenty, and I now knew that if I didn't get into professional baseball soon, I never would. Therefore, when Al Spink, a columnist on *The Sporting News*, told me he was willing to recommend me for an opening on the Terre Haute club in the Three-Eye League (Indiana, Illinois, Iowa), I asked him to go ahead. The team manager was Three-Fingers Brown, a former Cub pitcher who had been a hero of mine. The

day I showed up for work, Brown studied me incredu-
lously and asked: "You're a catcher?"

"Yes, sir, I am," I said.

"You look more like a jockey," he said.

I said: "Put a uniform on me and I'll show you."

I soon learned there was a lot I had to prove on this
team. In those days, a team at this level carried only
thirteen men, so when a new man was hired, somebody
else had to go, and the fellow leaving had more friends
than the man coming in. Though I was on the team, I
had to put up a real fight before I actually made the
team. During infield practice, for example, the fellows
would try to make me look bad by how and where they
threw the ball at me, sending me scurrying all over the
place. As in the Marines, I found I had to fight to stay
alive, and now I had to make myself look better by
working harder and harder. I was playing pretty good
ball, but it was killing me. As a matter of fact, you had
to be willing to face death if you wanted to play ball
in those days.

In one game, for example, the opposing team had a
man on third, and they needed this run very badly.
Manager Brown walked out to the mound and signalled
me to join him and the pitcher there, and he said:
"Now, Pepper, I want you to watch yourself. That guy
on third is going to try to score on anything, and it
won't bother him much if you are in the way. He out-
weighs you by at least a hundred pounds, so all I want
to tell you is do the best you can."

As I returned to the plate, I knew I was in trouble. If the next batter got a hit, we were sunk, of course. But even if he didn't hit safely, I knew he would try to send that ball out as far as he could. The runner would wait until it was caught, tag up, and then take off for home—and me. Then anything could happen. This time, the batter sent a fly ball out to the centerfielder. Out of the corner of one eye I saw the runner tag up, and at the same time I was trying to keep an eye on the ball on its way in to me. Later they told me what happened. That runner hit me and he hit me hard and he put me out of the game.

Looking back, this was a typical example of free enterprise as it is widely practiced. That guy had a right to hit me. I was in his way. I didn't have the ball. Standing there in his path was sheer stupidity. But I learned my lesson. A while later, the same situation came up again. This time, I called the huddle and I asked the third-baseman to come in on it.

I said to him: "Now, I've got a situation here that gave me some bad times back-a-ways, so listen. If this batter does hit a fly ball, you will be standing right behind that guy on third as he tags up. I want you to put your finger in the loop of his belt, and when he starts out, you just pull back a little. This will upset him for at least a couple of seconds and it may mean the difference between life and death as far as I am concerned."

We had only one umpire in those days and we kept him busy. I can remember seeing a man hit a ball and

head for first while the umpire was busy watching another play and after tagging first the guy took off
through the pitcher's box to third and nobody could
figure out how he got there. Since he was on our team,
I wasn't about to say anything. So I wasn't worried
about the umpire this time. The batter flied out to deep
left-center. Ready for the play at the plate, the umpire
was watching the ball. I glanced at third and saw the
runner tag up. Just as he was about to take off, he
seemed to stop in mid-air, so I knew the baseman had
him by the belt. It slowed him down long enough for
the ball to get the jump on him. It came in fast and
good and I had it in plenty of time for the slide. Ordinarily I would have tagged the runner on his feet, but
this time I decided to tag him in the mouth. This was
how I found out that you can get a baseball into a man's
mouth if you push hard enough. This was free enterprise, too.

It was a rough business. For me, the nights were
equally rough. I was homesick. As a nondrinker, I was
dull company, and to me nothing was duller than the
company of drunks, so there wasn't much for me to do
evenings but mope around hotel rooms and think about
Lil. Moreover, I had experienced a disappointment.
Three-Fingers Brown was a fine man; he had been a
great ballplayer and was eventually enrolled in the Hall
of Fame at Cooperstown, New York, and I looked forward to learning a lot about baseball from him. But
by the time I went to work for him he had passed his

prime and was no longer the athlete he had been, which was something of a letdown for me.

Then he let me know he wasn't too happy about me, either. One day in Terre Haute, right field was so drenched in a blinding sun that the rightfielder couldn't see a fly ball coming at him until it hit him on the head and knocked him out. Brown sent a pitcher out to replace the injured man. The pitcher also lost the ball in the sun. It struck him on the shoulder and almost paralyzed him. Glancing over at the bench, Brown saw me and asked: "Pepper, how about you in right field?"

I said: "Brownie, I'm sorry, but I'm a catcher and I can't play the outfield, certainly not a sun field."

He didn't say anything. He sent in another man and the game went on. That evening we traveled by train to Chicago, en route to play the team at Moline, Illinois, and as we were moving along, Brown sat down next to me. Calmly but very definitely he let me know that I was going to have to become a jack-of-all-trades if I wanted to stay on the ball club. There was enough threat in his voice to suggest that he didn't think this would be for very long. My spirits sank even lower. I had written Lil that we'd be passing through town and she was waiting for me at the Polk Street Station with a box of home-made fudge. I took one look at her standing there and suddenly I didn't care about anything or anybody else in the world. I touched her arm and said: "C'mon, I'm not going to Moline."

Jumping the club was a bad thing because it blacklisted me in organized baseball. Fortunately, friends were able to get me reinstated, and the following year a Chicago pitcher and I went out as a battery to a team in the South Dakota League. Shortly after our arrival we had offers of more money from an independent team. For this reason, the pitcher and I decided we would do better in what was called outlaw baseball, which was a group of teams that played each other more as a sporting event than as league competition leading to any sort of pennant. The team we joined was owned by a banker. Things went well until near the end of the season, when I badly injured a finger while making a bare-handed stab at a wild pitch. It bothered me a lot and put me on the bench.

Depressed, I began to give my standing in baseball some serious thought. My dream had always been to make the Big Leagues. I was now getting on in years and none of the major teams were chasing me with contracts. I faced the sad fact that I probably wasn't Big League material. It was about time, I figured, for me to settle down. I quit the team, I withdrew my savings from the bank, and then I did something I had been wanting to do for a long time. I sent Lil a telegram telling her I was coming home. Before I could leave town, some of the fellows pointed out that there were only a few days left to the season, and they suggested that I hang around and we could all travel home together. I agreed. One morning we awoke and found out that the bank had folded and the banker had committed suicide. Salaries which the other fellows had in the bank were lost, and so my money went to buy train tickets for them. When I returned to Chicago, I was broke. The one good thing I had going for me was that Lil was there to meet me. A few weeks later we were married.

I gave baseball one more fling. Al Spink, the sports writer, managed to interest the St. Louis Browns in me. Instead of being summoned for spring training the following year, I was told to show up at Sox Park the first time the Browns were in town that season, and Jimmy Burke, the manager, would look me over. It rained most of the time the Browns were in town, and because there were several others trying out for the team, I had little opportunity to show my stuff. However, Burke suggested that I go down to one of the Browns' farm teams in the Piedmont League, but I didn't consider that a step forward and declined the offer. An offer came to manage a team in South Dakota, but that would have been a step backward. Though I gave up the dream, I never lost the desire, but after that I limited my ball-playing to the Chicago semipro teams.

With my wife and my mother now both dependent on me, it was necessary for me to find a job. I knew I couldn't stand a nine-to-five job for long, and I didn't want a job where I'd have to sweat out a raise every other Christmas. By now I felt it was time that I started getting ahead in this world, and I wanted a job where my income would depend on individual performance, where I could go as far as I wished depending on how hard I was willing to work. I'd had some experience in selling while working for the paper company, so I decided that selling would be the best place for me to start. After making a study of the various things available in Chicago for me to sell, I chose insurance.

Looking back, I'm glad I did this. I had little business experience; I had no idea about business ethics or the lack of them; I was ignorant of the extent to which some salesmen would go to close a deal. Customer-stealing, commission-cutting, minimizing the importance of the small print—all these were tricks of the trade I learned after becoming the victim of them several times. I learned, too, that, in most instances, loyalty to the firm was a dollars-and-cents affair, as the firm's loyalty to the salesman usually was. It was a cutthroat racket, and if I went into it naïve I didn't remain so for long. Once I had my eyes opened, I knew what to watch for. If I managed to survive, it was mostly because baseball had made me fast on my feet and, enjoying the competition more than I despised the double-dealing, I was willing to work longer and harder than the next guy.

Early in selling I learned the wisdom in the story about the man who commented about a successful friend: "Isn't Joe lucky?" And a bystander said: "Yes, and the harder he works the luckier he gets." I had my best luck working hard in an area others overlooked because it seemed so unpromising. Every noon I'd go to some factory and start a conversation, usually about baseball, with the men as they were having their lunch. I learned early that men usually shied away from the topic of life insurance, so I saved it for last. Instead, I'd guide the talk around to the subject of savings, suggesting that it was important for a man to have some money in the bank in the event of some emergency. Everybody agreed with that, of course, and they also agreed that it was often difficult for a working man to keep any money in the bank once he put it there because there always seemed to be emergencies coming up. Then I would broach the subject of life insurance as a form of savings. Since insurance was a family matter, any interested man would tell me he'd talk it over with his wife, and I would try to persuade him to let me do the talking. This was the way I got evening appointments in the home. I found that appointments were extremely difficult to line up, but once I got one, I usually made the sale.

I'd been in the insurance business about four years when, returning to the office late one night, I found a note from another salesman, a man named Evans, asking me to meet him the next day at an address up on the North Side. I figured he was about to sell a big one and wanted some moral support as he moved in, so I went up there. When the lady of the house answered my knock, I identified myself and I said I was looking for my friend. She said: "Oh, yes, he's out in the kitchen." I thought that was a strange place to sell insurance, but I realized that each man must work out a system that's best for him and I assumed this was his. When I got to the kitchen, I saw that a few other women were there, and there was Evans with an apron tied around him. He was at the stove cooking a meal. I was about to ask him if he'd already finished the laundry, when he took me aside and explained what was going on.

It was a new way to sell aluminum pots and pans, by means of home demonstrations. A prospective customer was asked to invite several of her friends to her home for a free lunch—to be provided, cooked and served by the salesman in her own kitchen. Immediately I recognized this as a great idea, with real potential for growth. What better way was there to prove your claims for a product than by putting it to the test before its severest critics—housewives? After enjoying a lunch they didn't have to prepare or clean up after, the women were open to the sales pitch, and each in turn became a prospective customer who had the privilege of inviting other friends to her home for a demonstration, and free lunch. For me, this technique solved the whole problem of appointments in the selling business.

Evans explained that he had already given several demonstrations, had made sales that surprised even him, and that he was about to quit the insurance business. He said: "Pepper, I think you can sell this stuff. And it's a new business. The field is wide open."

I was sure I could sell the line, so I went to the company's office and signed up. The market was opening so fast that the company couldn't find enough men with selling experience. The man who tried to break me in had been driving a cab two weeks before. With four years of insurance selling behind me, I felt I could handle that side of the business. What I had to learn was how to give the demonstration. At this point of my life, I couldn't even boil an egg, so it wasn't surprising that on my first demonstration I burned all the food. When I got home that night, I told Lil that I was taking over the kitchen for a while, which she didn't mind at all. When, after two or three more bad tries, I finally got the thing down, I gave the kitchen back to her. For some reason, she didn't mind that either.

After two or three months, I started getting complaints from some of my early customers. With frequent use, the pots and pans were undergoing a discoloration, affecting the taste of the food. I came to the conclusion that I was handling an inferior product. Meanwhile, another company had come into the same business. I examined their products and found them to be excellent. Knowing I would feel better selling a line I could have faith in, I applied for a job with this company and was hired.

Then a tragedy struck that sank me to the lowest point of my life. It was March 1926. Lil and I had our daughter Mary, a fine young lady of three years, and we were expecting another child. Since I was on a new job, we knew there wouldn't be much money coming in for a while, and to economize we moved from our nice apartment into a basement flat that was a horrible place. Business didn't improve, and we were soon completely broke.

I had a car that had been driven a great many miles and would blow a head-gasket at the least provocation. It seemed to know just when I couldn't afford it. One morning I spent the last of our money on food for a luncheon demonstration to a group of women to whom I hoped to sell cooking utensils. The appointment was in one of the western suburbs. The weather was rotten; the ground was covered with a couple of feet of snow. I made the trip out in terror and discouragement.

The demonstration went well, however, and I got nine sales appointments for the next day. I returned home still in terror but now with a little optimism. I reached home late and discovered that my wife had been rushed to the hospital. By the time I got there the baby had died, and Lil was in such serious shape I was not allowed to see her. I blamed myself for everything. If I had been a decent provider, my family wouldn't have to live in such horrible conditions and my wife would have an easier life. I sat up all night punishing myself. I had never felt so low.

By dawn, I realized that it was crucially urgent for me to prove to Lil that I was not a failure, and the only way for me to do that was to hustle. I was at my first appointment at 7:30 A.M. and when I finished the day many hours later I had earned $450 in commissions, most of it in cash. I hurried to the hospital and showed

Lil the money and my orders, and I promised her that never again would I let our lives get into such a mess. She smiled a little, trying to make her pride in me overcome the pain we both felt because of the loss of the baby. I kept right on hustling, with the result that a few months later I was offered the assistant managership of the St. Louis office. I took it because I wanted to get my family away from the sad memories Chicago held. A year later, I was put in charge of the Cleveland office. I was not a Christian during this period and I had no idea that tragedies, like blessings, can be part of God's plans for a man. As things improved, I merely felt that Lil and I had come through another of life's experiences. I didn't know that God was moving me along.

A special advantage our salesman had was that the product was not available in stores. I suppose somebody at the main office decided the company was missing a good bet because, after I had been in Cleveland about two years, the company decided to put out a similar line to be sold in stores. It was a less expensive line and, as I found out when I examined samples, an inferior product that wasn't what the company claimed it to be. I complained to the head office that not only would going into stores wreck the present effective system of selling through home demonstrations but also sooner or later the inferior line would damage the reputation of the original product. All that came out of this was a company offer for me to supervise selling of the second line to stores in the San Francisco area. I turned it down, and the next thing I knew I was back in Chicago and out of a job.

I didn't know where to turn for a job. Looking back, I know now that the job I eventually found provided a turning point in my life. It put me on the road that ultimately led me to the Lord.

CHOOSE PATHS
THAT GO PLACES

Looking back on your life can be like making a quilt. You start out with a lot of memories of unrelated events which occurred at unrelated times, but as you sew the patches together you recognize a distinct pattern. You see that something that happened to you this morning gives perspective and meaning to something that happened years ago, and the reverse can be equally true. For me, this is a way of perceiving God's guidance in my life. Too many seemingly unrelated events have occurred in my life for any other explanation.

My new job was a case in point. I needed a job. I had a wife and two children to support, so I couldn't afford to shop around. I considered myself a salesman and intended to remain one, but an event had occurred which made my prospects rather gloomy. It was late 1929, the stock market had crashed, and there weren't many people around with enough money to do much buying of anything. This alone should have discouraged me from taking the job I did.

In the course of job-hunting, I heard about a new company in the business of mothproofing homes and offices. I didn't know a thing about moths. The only times I'd ever given moths a thought were when I saw one. But now I found myself extremely interested in them. It wasn't a matter of the job, it would never have occurred to me to look for a job in this field. I simply got interested in moths. The interest was, I now believe, a matter of guidance. God stirred the interest not merely so that I could get a job but because of other plans He had for me in the years ahead.

When I went down to the company to find out if there was a place for me in it, the man who owned the organization offered to sell me a franchise covering part of Chicago. I was broke. A car I had purchased in Cleveland was about to be repossessed. I was in no position to invest in a business, nor did I care to. But I offered to sell on commission, and they agreed. I met the two men who were doing the production work. They had bought into the company but weren't too happy about it because there wasn't much work to do.

In order to know what I was talking about, I found out all I could about moths and our product, and I found out that the moths didn't have too much to worry about. There wasn't, in fact, a single product on the market that could do more than a superficial job on moth eggs and larvae, which were the real problems, and most of them were effective only against those moth flies who wanted to commit suicide by wallowing in a puddle of the stuff. Repeatedly prospective customers complained that previous mothproofing had been effective only a short time, if at all, and many expressed the opinion that mothproofing really didn't work. I couldn't blame the prospects for being reluctant. It was, after all, a matter of "buyer beware," and with the Depression in its first months, people were being very careful with their money. I felt, however, that our product, though not perfect, was better than most, but I needed some way to prove it. Also it seemed to me that we could do with a little "seller beware" by having the company shoulder some of the responsibility. I therefore worked out a plan whereby the company would guarantee its work for a specific period. But I didn't get a chance to talk to the boss about it. One morning I showed up at the office to get my assignments for the day and I saw the other fellows loitering in the corridor outside the locked door. We eventually learned that the man who ran the outfit had taken off, leaving only the unpaid bills behind.

I was surprised but not shocked. I had already discovered that the business world was a place where everybody had to beware. Not even employees were safe. For example, when I was selling insurance, I realized I could do a better job if I had a car. I had some money in the bank but I needed another $500 to pay cash for the car and avoid financing costs. I talked the matter over with my boss, who agreed to lend me the money to be repaid at $50 a month. A few months later, I received a very good offer from another agency. Because I was young, new in the business and didn't have any older friend who could advise me, I decided to talk over the offer with my boss. He hit the ceiling. He called me an ingrate and a blackmailer, and he accused me of using the offer as bait for a raise to cover the payments on the car. I tried to explain that all I wanted to know was my chances for future advancement with him before considering the offer, but I couldn't get a word in. I took the other job, and I continued the monthly payments on the car. In fact, I was downstairs in the bank writing out a money order for another payment one day when a man who worked in the building identified me to a process server. I learned that I was being sued for defaulting on a loan that was repayable on demand. In court, I told my story and then my ex-boss's lawyer told his, saying that he had documentation in his office to show I had signed a demand note. I didn't even know what a demand note was and said so to the judge. The judge suggested that I take a look at it and let him know the outcome. I walked to the office with the lawyer, an elderly man who, on the way, gave me a stern, fatherly lecture on clean living and starting life on the right foot. The documentation turned out to be the canceled check, and under my endorsement someone had typed: "Payable on demand." I knew the words hadn't been there when I signed the check, and I did my best to convince the judge of this. He assured me he would investigate the situation, adding that if I didn't hear from him in a couple of weeks, I could forget the matter. I didn't hear from him, but sometime later I did hear that both my old boss and his lawyer had been forced out of business. Maybe that's the way the Lord handled it.

And He does handle these things. The Lord will have His justice, which is something that should be kept in mind not only in fear of the Lord but out of love for Him. If a man hasn't as yet learned to love God enough, the Bible can give him plenty of reasons for obeying Him out of fear. In Acts 5, we can see how swiftly the Lord's justice sometimes operates, when a property owner by the name of Ananias made the mistake of trying to hold out on the Apostle Peter. In those days, Christians used their private holdings for the good of the brethren. Apparently, there was a need for some ready cash because Ananias offered to sell a piece of his land to raise the money. After he sold the plot, he had a little talk with his wife and they agreed to keep some of the money for themselves without telling anybody about it. They must have been quite a pair.

When Ananias went to the meeting place, he tried to create the impression that he was handing in all the money. But Peter, who could discern people's thoughts, said: "Ananias, why have you let Satan tempt you into trying to lie to the Holy Spirit by holding back part of the price of the land? That land was yours; when you sold it, the money was yours, and it was your idea to give all the money to the brethren. Why are you trying to pretend that you have done so? You are not lying to me—you're lying to God." Before Ananias could say a word, he was struck dead. Some men carried him out and buried him. A few hours later, his wife showed up, and Peter asked her: "Sapphira, isn't it true that Ananias sold that land for more than he turned in?" She admitted it was true, and Peter said: "Those men over there just buried your husband and now they are going to bury you." And she dropped dead.

If God struck people dead every time they cheated, we wouldn't be faced with a population explosion these days. I've heard people say that they can't believe that a loving God could also be a vengeful God, but I suspect that this is wishful thinking. The Bible is full of examples of the vengeance of the Lord, from Adam and Eve to the Deluge to the Tower of Babel, to name just a few. "To me belong vengeance and recompense," God said to Moses, and since God is Eternal He has all of eternity in which to even the score.

If a businessman remembered this, he wouldn't have to think twice when offered a chance to make a fast buck on a shady deal, whether it's the quality of his product, the thoroughness of his service, the size of his markup, the terms of his contract or beating the competition. Even if he takes the chance and gets away with the deal, he hasn't gained anything in the long run. We don't seem to have many mind readers like Peter around these days so it's possible for us to lie to the brethren, but we can't lie to God. Forgetting this was what cost Ananias and Sapphira their lives. We all pay the same price, one way or another, when we forget. Sometimes when we hear about men like that boss of mine who was forced out of business, we're inclined to say: "Well, he got *his*." But we overlook the fact that in trying to get along without the Lord we may be getting ours less severely in those numerous troubles that plague us every day and we don't know why. Only when we learn to consult the Lord daily through His messages in the Bible will we see those troubles disappear.

The morning I found the door locked at the mothproofing company, I had some new troubles of my own. Besides losing my job, that Hupmobile I bought in Cleveland had just been repossessed. Not only did I have nowhere to go but I had no way to get there. As bad off as I was, the other fellows who had put money into the company by buying franchises and equipment were in worse shape. I got talking to one of them, and as we were sympathizing with each other, a thought struck me. Just because the company had gone out of business was no reason that this fellow and I had to. I had learned that I could sell the mothproofing service and he knew that he could do the job. When I suggested that he stay with me and handle the production, he was all for it. The willingness of the chemical com-

71

pany which made the cleaning material to extend credit to us until we got rolling was a great encouragement to us.

The only trouble was that I needed a car. At a used-car lot near my home in Oak Park, I came upon a Ford that was going for $90, but they insisted on cash, which I didn't have. The morning after the franchise-holder and I decided to go into business for ourselves, I faced the fact that there would be very little business unless I was able to move around to find it. Unable to move far that morning, I left the apartment and started canvassing the immediate neighborhood. For a couple of hours nothing happened, and then I came upon an elderly couple sunning themselves on their front porch on the crisp spring morning. I went up to them, introduced myself and began making my pitch. The woman said she didn't worry about moths at this time of the year. I tried to assure her that housewives should worry about moth eggs the whole year round. To this she said that she was a good housekeeper and she was certain that there were no such things in her house. I suggested that she could have complete peace of mind if she'd let me take a look around. The place was loaded. Amazed, as housewives always are when they discover the infestation, she was sold, and, like a good housewife, the only question she had left was how much would the job cost. I blurted out the figure that had been haunting me: $90. Thus, with the first sale I made as a self-employed man, I got myself a car.

To be sure, I still had my troubles, and some of these were on my mind a few months later when, with Mother, I went to Moody Church and heard the sermon about the Bible that made a Christian out of me. Yet even this experience was not enough to give me the sense to recognize that the Lord was showing me the way if I would just open my eyes. This didn't happen until I had almost lost my eyes.

My partner and I remained in business for the remainder of 1930. The next year, I went up to Milwaukee to introduce mothproofing as a service for a warehousing company, but when the outfit refused to invest the capital necessary to build a staff, I returned to Chicago and went into business with an exterminator. At this point, I was not only soliciting business but I was doing the work as well.

Frequently, people would ask me where moths came from. They came from the same place people did. God made them. "In the beginning God created . . ." That is how the Bible begins. By experience, I have found that a great many problems are settled for me if I accept, by faith, that sovereign statement. But don't ask me why God created moths. It might have been so that the Wades could eat occasionally, but surely He had other reasons. Moths are scavengers. They will eat anything that has ever been alive. In the forests, naturalists have found that moths have devoured the corpses of dead animals, especially those with long hair, so maybe they were meant to do the undertaking.

In my business, I was still using the mothproofing method of that short-lived company, and I was still dissatisfied with it. A businessman's best advertisement is a satisfied customer, and when the customers are calling you up a few months later and asking you to come over and see the damage done by the moths you were supposed to have killed, you can tell they're not satisfied. I was doing the best I could. It was the process that wasn't good enough. Even so, the responsibility was mine and I felt I had to do something about it.

I tried other products and blends of other products but there was no improvement because the approach was wrong. For example, the only way you can kill a moth with mothballs is to hit him over the head with one. Flakes and crystals won't hurt him at all. People think it's the strong smell of these substances that kills moths or keeps them away, whereas the truth is that moths don't have a sense of smell. The smell, however, can keep your neighbors away, if that's what you want. Some of these products do give off fatal fumes in the form of a heavy gas, but for this to be effective you would have to put about twenty pounds of the stuff on the top shelf of the closet and then seal off the closet for as long as three months. Aerosol bombs, contact sprays, even sprays containing poisons are ineffective not only because they depend on contact but because they can't be sold in sufficiently toxic concentration for the contact to be fatal after a short time. When I'm asked why these products are in the stores, the only explanation I have is that they're in stores because people buy them. In turn, people buy them because the stores sell them.

The situation always reminds me of the man who was visiting an Army base one day and came upon a soldier standing next to a cannon and carefully studying his wristwatch. The man asked what was going on, and the soldier explained: "At six o'clock on the nose every evening, I fire this cannon, the flag is lowered, and our workday is over." The man asked how the soldier could be so sure that it was always six on the nose, and the soldier said: "There's a jewelry store in town that has a very expensive clock in the window, and I know that the jeweler takes expert care of it. So every day when I'm in town, I set my watch by that clock." Later, the man happened to pass the jewelry shop and he went in for a look at that clock, mentioning that he'd heard that the jeweler took such good care of it. "Oh, yes," the jeweler said. "Every evening at six o'clock on the nose they fire a cannon over at the Army base, and if this clock is off I adjust it."

My opportunity to set the clock correctly occurred in the form of one of those unexpected, unrelated episodes which some people call fate or coincidence but which I call guidance—another patch for the quilt. One day in 1932, I was working in a home in Evanston and, as usually happened, got into a conversation with the lady of the house about moths. She was really interested and asked a lot of intelligent questions. She remarked

how strange it was that nobody had done enough sci-
entific research on moths to develop a substance which
would do a thorough job of killing them. To this I
said that if I could get into a good laboratory I would
certainly do the research myself. She told me that she
had a friend in a high position at Northwestern University and offered to find out if I could use a laboratory
there. I thanked her, but I couldn't believe that Northwestern University would open its laboratory to a research scientist of my qualifications. To my surprise,
this fine woman telephoned me a few days later with
the news that I had an appointment with her friend. To
my greater surprise, I talked to this man only a few
minutes, explaining what I wanted to do, when he picked
up a telephone, called a professor who headed one of
the biology laboratories and told him to give me free
range and full cooperation.

For a period of several months, I was at the laboratory
practically every day, studying generation after generation of moths and trying to find some way to destroy
them in the egg and larva stages. I knew that killing the
eggs would be difficult because often they are deposited
in crevices and under the woodwork where most fumes
don't penetrate. The larvae presented a problem, too.
The moth larva breathes through pores. When dis-
turbed in any way, the larva closes the pores, curls up
into a tight ball and can remain this way for hours without apparently taking in any air at all. And during the
cocoon stage, a moth is as safe as if he were in a Sher-

man tank. After experimenting with dozens of different materials, I was finally able to develop a substance that when heated gave off a heavy, toxic gas which, as pressure was created through accumulation in a sealed area, could not only penetrate the deep hiding places where the moth thought she had safely laid her eggs but also had a staying power longer than any larva could hold its breath, longer than any pupa could remain in its cocoon. I called the substance Fumakill, and for many years it paid my rent. Then the day came when it almost killed me.

It was a morning in 1944. I was mothproofing a closet in a Wheaton, Illinois, home when the chemicals exploded in my face. Most of the next year I spent in hospitals, and that year gave me time to think. All I could think of at first was that I was lucky to be alive, lucky even though the doctors believed I would probably lose my vision. Blind, I wouldn't be able to work, at least not the way I used to. But I had my business and I felt I could still run it. Vernon Anderson, who was working for me, was a good man and I figured that in the future I could solicit new business by telephone and he could go out and do it. Resigning myself to the new life I would have to learn to live, I waited in the darkness for the day when the doctors would tell me I could get going again.

Then the doctors discovered that I would not be blind. More months of bandages and inactivity were ahead but eventually, the doctors said, I would be myself again. I was not sure I wanted that. With nothing to do but think, I had reflected a great deal on my life, about how it shaped up to this point, and I was not satisfied. I was barely making ends meet, but this wasn't what bothered me. Though the business was gradually expanding, I somehow sensed that as a man I was standing still. The business occupied most of my time, and I found myself wondering whether I was the type who worked to live or lived to work. Either way, the whole thing seemed pointless. I had almost lost my life; now that it was mine again, I wanted to do more with it than I had done. The gnawing feeling that I was missing something haunted me, but I had no idea what I was lacking so I didn't know where to begin to look for it.

I knew, of course, that accidents can happen. But I also knew that sometimes the Lord lets an accident happen for reasons of His own. I'm sure that Paul at first thought it was an accident when he fell off his horse on his way to Damascus to persecute the Christians, but then he found out that the Lord had knocked him off his horse in the process of making a Christian of him. I was already a Christian. I had been reborn, I had given my life to God, and I now figured that if my accident was God's way of trying to get through to me on some point He would eventually let me know what it was. I kept wondering what it might be.

After my bandages were removed, I wasn't allowed to read much. But all I wanted to read was my Bible. Since my conversion, the Bible had become very important to me. I read it, I taught it, I felt I was familiar with it. But I already knew that each time I picked up my Bible I found something new, not because I hadn't read a particular passage before but because previously the passage had no special significance or application for me. This was why I considered it necessary to read the Bible regularly. A man's life changes, he moves into new situations, he gets to see things differently, he sees himself differently, and if he hopes to have any understanding of what is happening around him the best place for him to look is to the source of all understanding—the Bible. Certainly something had happened to me. I had survived an accident that should have killed me. And not only had I survived, but I had come out of it in pretty good shape. I had the doctors to thank for this, but I also knew it was God who supplied the doctors.

This was on my mind as I began to page through my Bible. I came upon the Book of Joshua, which I had read more than once. It caught my interest and I found myself desiring to read it again. In the first chapter, verse eight, I came upon this:

"This book of the law shall not depart out of thy mouth; but thou shalt meditate therein day and night, that thou mayest observe to do according to all that is written therein: for then thou shalt make thy way prosperous, and then thou shalt have good success."

The words struck me as an outright order, but I wondered how anyone could obey it. Meditate on the Bible

79

day and night? How would I get any work done? Or could it mean that I was supposed to keep the Bible in mind day and night? The words "that thou mayest observe to do according to all that is written therein" were clear enough. The whole purpose of reading the Bible and keeping it in mind was to learn how to conduct ourselves and our daily affairs. The remaining phrases seemed to be promises: if I knew the Bible and lived by the Bible I would experience prosperity and success. I discovered later that this was the only place in the Bible where the word "success" appears—and it is used in reference to the use of the Bible itself.

Reflecting on this verse, I felt I was doing my best to live according to the Bible, doing so out of my love for God, my desire to obey Him and please Him. I wanted His blessings. I expected them. But if prosperity and success were blessings, I knew I wasn't getting much. I read on and, in Chapter 24, Joshua, found:

"Choose you this day whom ye will serve . . . as for me and my house, we will serve the Lord."

This, too, required some reflection. As far as "me and my house" were concerned, I knew that the Lord was being served by everyone in my home. And yet it seemed to me that Joshua was addressing the heads of the tribes of Israel. Joshua, successor to Moses, had led the Israelites into Canaan where, after conquering the pagans who were living there, he apportioned the land to the tribes to use for their farming. Evidently the paganism had made some inroads, for Joshua told the leaders to make a choice of serving the Lord or the pagan gods. Then he told them where he stood. In my dictionary, the word "serve" has twenty definitions, and the first is "to work for." Joshua worked for the Lord as he led the Israelites into the Promised Land, he worked for the Lord as he led his people into victorious battle, and now that the fighting was over he was going to continue working for the Lord in building a nation. A lot of people would help him—the people of his house: his advisers, his subordinates, his family, even the men who plowed his fields. Working for him, they were also working for the Lord. The Book of Joshua states:

"And Israel served the Lord all the days of Joshua, and all the days of the elders that outlived Joshua, and which had known all the works of the Lord, that he had done for Israel."

This made me think of the companies I knew which had had Christian management or Christian ownership, and as long as things remained that way I felt I was able to do business with these companies without worrying about being robbed. But then, either through retirement or death, the Christian left the scene, and things changed. I had to be careful again about reading the small print. Occasionally these Christian men would tell me that they believed God was guiding them, but when the man left his company so, evidently, did the guidance. Unlike the elders who outlived Joshua, some people in the company couldn't have known what the Lord had done.

I found myself wondering what the Lord would do with a company that was entirely His, a company in which every employee, from top to bottom, did his job for the glory of God. In the first Book of Samuel, God says: "Them that honor me, I will honor." I was trying personally to honor God, but I had never tried this with my company because I had been trained in the school of competition which attests that religion and business don't mix. In other words, I was ready enough to meditate on the Book of the Law by night, but not by day.

An idea began to grow in me, and I found myself getting excited about something for the first time in months. I had a few men working with me who had been boys in my Bible class after my conversion and who had come to me looking for a job after they finished school. They were fine young men; I knew they were Christians; we had prayed together, but over individual matters. I was confident they would pray with me as fellow-workers in a company dedicated entirely to the Lord.

I closed my eyes and I prayed. I told the Lord that I loved Him and that I trusted in His love for the forgiveness of my neglects. I pledged that there and then I was committing myself to Him entirely—myself, my homes, my business—day and night. I would turn everything over to Him. I said: "I don't expect any miracles. I

don't intend to sit back and expect You to run everything, but I want You to tell me how to run things and
to send my way the men I will need to do the job. I
realize that all I have to know is in the Bible and I will
seek it, but I will need Your help to understand it. I
choose to serve the Lord, but You will have to show me
how."

I did not do this lightly. I knew that I might well
be asking for trouble. After all, in business I did not
deal entirely with reborn persons, and I realized that
the time would come when I would have to make decisions which could cost the company money and progress rather than do anything that was against the Lord.
Moreover, I didn't want this commitment to be a secret
between God and me, nor did I want it to be a secret
shared only with the men working with me. I wanted
everybody in on it, openly, in the company and in the
community, even though I knew a lot of people wouldn't
want to do business with what they considered a pack
of religious nuts. And I wanted something more. I
wanted to have men working with me who would know
what the Lord had done, and was doing, because with
such men I knew that, as the Lord was receiving me
into His glory, I would be able to tell Him that His
company was still working for Him.

When I opened my eyes after my prayer, I caught
myself smiling. I was truly full of joy. I didn't feel relief.
On the contrary, I realized I had taken on a great respon-

sibility and I was very much aware of it. But I had purpose now. I had meaning. I had direction.

And I was soon to learn that when you ask the Lord for His counsel He not only shows you how to do the job but also gives you the tools.

▪ ▪ ▪ 5 ▪ ▪ ▪

CHRISTIAN VITALITY AND TEAMWORK MAKE BUSINESS A MINISTRY

When you go to work for the Lord you find yourself raising the level of your efforts. Your job becomes more than a job. It becomes a calling. It is now the ministry by which you glorify God. You work harder and you do a better job so that your efforts will please the Lord who is now your silent partner. To acknowledge Him as your Lord is simply to say that He is now your boss. He watches, judges, knows when we are doing the job and when we are merely looking busy. When we are aware of this, when we openly acknowledge it, when that's the way we want it to be, our lives take vitality and meaning. And we should want to have this kind of relationship.

"Seek that ye may excel," Paul instructed the Corinthians. In other words, do your best and then try to do better because the pursuit of excellence is the hallmark of a Christian who knows that God is measuring him every minute not only by his prayers but by his deeds as well. The man who does his job to draw his pay, then maybe works a little harder when he's about to ask for a raise, really isn't worth much because he has a short-range view of his whole life. Two of the most decisive Biblical admonitions I've come across are in Paul's letter to the Colossians, when he says: "Set your affection on things above, not on things on the earth," and "Whatsoever you do in word or deed, do all in the name of the Lord Jesus, giving thanks to God and the Father by Him." That's the long-range view, and it's the only attitude that matters.

The man who possesses this attitude can be spotted a mile away because he effuses the best single ingredient a man can have: vitality. I once looked up that word and was amazed by the scope of its meanings—fundamental, basic, essential, necessary, needful, significant, truth, animation, living, exuberant, of critical importance, imparting life and vigor, something having vital force. I thought the definition was being stretched a bit but I wondered: "Does the word 'vitality' actually mean 'possessing truth of critical importance,' and is this applicable to the business world or is it limited to the clergy?"

Then I remembered my personal reaction when as a young man in the insurance business I settled my first death claim. I realized that through my business of advising and counseling in the sale of that policy I had rendered a tremendous service to a family that soon needed it desperately. What I had said to them was

86

truth and it was of vital importance. This was the event that made me a missionary for the insurance business. Similarly, I became a missionary again when I started selling aluminum ware. I could truthfully say the product was the best on the market and it was important to the family because it allowed the housewife to cook meals easier and better and with more healthful results. Had the company kept faith with those of us doing the selling instead of competing with us by going into stores, I perhaps might still be selling that product because I was very proud of it. In each of these instances, however, my zeal was earthbound, different from the God-centered vitality of a ministry. It wasn't until I committed my life entirely to the Lord that I realized how big the difference could be.

When a man commits himself to the Lord, there is no longer any room in his life for creeping indifference because he is constantly aware of God's vitalizing presence. The excitement in living for the Lord is tremendous. I know He is with me every minute, watching me, guiding me. Whenever a problem of any kind comes up, I consult with Him through prayer, meditation and the Bible. The decision is my own and I am responsible for it, but as long as I make it on His terms I know I have nothing to worry about. I know, too, that over the years people have been amused that among the things I turned over to God was a company that was in the business of killing moths, as though this were something odd to offer Him. Some years ago I ran across an apt poem in this regard; I don't know who the author is but he certainly knew what he was talking about when he wrote:

Every mason in the quarry, every builder on the shores,
Every chopper in the forest, every raftsman at the oar,
Hewing wood and drawing water, splitting stones and cleaving sod,
All the dusty ranks of labor in the regiments of God
March together toward His triumph, do the tasks His hands prepare.
Honest toil is holy service. Faithful work is praise and prayer.

That's about as neatly as it can be put. Moreover, if the Lord Himself was willing to dignify hard labor by working as a carpenter, any one of us can bring dignity to our job, whatever it is, by dedicating our efforts to His glory. Commitment is an opportunity open to all men at any level in any kind of work.

I felt the change immediately. I had a small business then, operating out of my home, and when I was able to return to work I told the fellows with me about my commitment. As I expected, they joined me in it completely. Thereafter, we began each day with a prayer and an acknowledgment of our commitment. In honoring the Lord we knew that He would honor us if He were satisfied with us, and we sought nothing more. Deuteronomy warns: "Ye shall not tempt the Lord your God. . . . Ye shall diligently keep the commandments of the Lord your God, and his testimonies, and his statutes, which he hath commanded thee. And thou shalt do that which is right and good in the sight of the Lord: that it may be well with thee, and that thou mayest go in and possess the good land which the Lord sware unto thy fathers." (Deut. 6:16, 17, 18). So now that we were in business with the Lord we weren't worried about Him holding up His end but just about holding up ours.

We all felt the influence. We found ourselves undergoing changes in our attitudes toward each other as well as toward the job. We all got along better; there was more willingness to go the extra mile, to work the extra hour; and when disagreement arose, as it inevitably does, we were able to resolve it by a prompt discussion rather than carry grudges and lose tempers. We respected each other more because we had more respect for ourselves, knowing and acknowledging ourselves to be creatures of God dedicated to His service. The dedication brought vitality into the group. We developed a new pride in doing a good job. Experience convinced us we truly had the best product on the market and we knew our work was important because of the thousands of dollars it would save a family.

Our own business family began to grow. After World War II, some of my former Bible students, returning from military duty, needed jobs, and I was happy to take about a dozen of them into the organization. We found an office near Belmont Avenue, a long, narrow store with a potbelly stove at the back. Every morning we gathered around the stove to begin our day in prayerful commitment, submitting ourselves to the Lord and His will. I often told the men: "We are in the mothproofing business because God wants us to be in the mothproofing business, and when He wants us to do anything else He will let us know." And that was exactly what happened.

Often when I'd be mothproofing a home, the lady of the house would ask me if I could recommend somebody to clean her rugs. I had developed a policy against making such recommendations. The two or three times I had suggested somebody, the job was badly done, and I heard about it from the customer. Afterward, when anyone asked the question, I'd reply: "Look in the Yellow Pages." As things were, the people in the rug-cleaning business were unwittingly contributing to mine. In the eating process, digestive fluids in the moth-larva's stomach change the animal fiber into a fatty albumoid which is assimilative. Rug-cleaners who use inferior soap-base materials leave behind coconut oil residues which, at room temperature, turn rancid and form fatty albumoids. This makes the fiber more digestible for the larva, it will eat more, the damage is more quickly noticeable, and out goes the cry for help to the mothproofers.

Also, wall-to-wall carpeting was becoming increasingly popular. It could be beautiful, of course, but the trouble with it was that it was inconvenient to send out for cleaning and sometimes it shrank and didn't fit right when it was replaced. I was aware of all these things but I didn't give them much thought until one night when I was working alone in a downtown office. Lunch-time came, and I went out to the reception room for a comfortable seat. As I ate, I paged through the magazines there, and I came upon an ad that seemed to stand out. It was in a magazine for the chemical industry, and this ad announced the development of a new mordant for the dyeing process. The substance was supposed to be able to penetrate fabric better than anything else. Penetration was a problem in rug cleaning. Getting the cleanser deep into the rug required a great amount of water, and this could cause the shrinkage. The thought crossed my mind that blending the mordant with a cleanser might be a good way to clean rugs without having to use so much water, or so much cleanser that it would leave a residue.

The thought passed. I finished the magazine and my lunch and returned to work. But every once in a while I found myself thinking about that ad. As I left the office, I stopped in the reception room for another look at the ad and to note the name of the manufacturer. I had no idea why I was doing this.

The family was asleep when I got home. I wanted to unwind a little, so I sat in the chair next to the end table on which the Bible lay. I picked up the book and began to read. I couldn't concentrate and I kept wondering what was wrong with me, when into my mind popped the question: "Why don't you experiment with that mordant yourself and try to develop a way to clean rugs on the floor in the home?" I knew as sure as I was sitting there that the idea was not my own. And at the same moment I knew it was a great idea, especially with wall-to-wall carpeting. That moment, I would have agreed that it couldn't be done, and yet the idea was too good to dismiss without giving it a chance. Moreover, when the chips fall into place like that, it means just one thing: the Lord is at work.

Why me? Why not me? Business is the ministry in which I serve the Lord, and if there is anything He wants done that is somewhat in my line it is reasonable that He should propose it. In the Scriptures we read about the businessmen who, before going on a long trip, called in three servants and gave them some money in talents, the coinage of the day. To one he gave five talents, to another he gave two, to the third he gave one. While he was away, the first two men invested their talents and doubled their principal, but the third man, afraid of how his boss would react if he invested his one talent unwisely, played safe and hid it in the ground. When the businessman returned, he summoned the three servants to find out what they had done with the money he had advanced them. He was very pleased with the first two and gave them promotions. Then the third man stepped up and said, "Well, I know how you are and I didn't want to lose this talent, so I buried it. Here it is back." The boss got angry and said, "If you didn't want to risk investing it, why didn't you at least lend it to somebody so we could get some interest back on it?" And he took the talent away, gave it to the man who had ten, and fired the man who had done nothing with his talent. Some exegetes interpret the "talent" as referring to the special abilities God gives to each man. If we don't use our talent, it may be taken away from us and we may be punished as well. If I have a talent for business, at least my business, it is because God gave it to me. Moreover, when I committed my life to the Lord I asked him to make me sensitive to His will. I believe He did, and I believe He expressed it that night regarding the rug cleanser. Why something as commonplace as a rug cleanser? Nothing is commonplace to God. I believe, too, that God tries to get through to us every day but we don't hear because we don't trust enough in His judgment, and so we bury our talents in the ground.

I wasn't about to bury mine. I went to the manufacturer of the mordant and got into a discussion about rug cleansers with one of the executives. He said the company already had a rug cleanser, one with a coconut oil soap containing ether. I explained to him why it wouldn't work, but he said the company was satisfied with it and people were buying it. This was the same hopeless cycle I had encountered in the mothproofing industry. I led the conversation around to the mordant and I explained the idea that God had given me. The man agreed that it sounded interesting and he said that the company would have no objections if I wanted to go ahead and try it out.

I did. I collected numerous samples of rug fabrics.

Then I spent weeks blending the mordant with various detergents which were free of vegetable oils, testing each mixture on the fabrics until I came up with a batch that appeared to be exceptionally effective. The next time a mothproofing customer asked me about having her rugs cleaned, I told her about the process I had developed. I warned her that I still considered it experimental. I was confident that it wouldn't harm her rugs, but I wasn't sure how good a job it would do. She told me to go ahead. It did an excellent job. After a few more such experiments, I felt ready to add the service to my mothproofing business.

We started to move ahead fast. I realized there was no limit to our growth potential and I faced the fact that if we were going to become a big organization I would need the help of men who had a better head for business than I did. Just as once I had to face the fact that I wasn't Big League material in baseball, I also had to admit that I had a lot to learn about merchandising. My experience with Fumakill taught me this. After I developed the device, I considered it simple enough for the average housewife to use without calling in professional help. I managed to sell a Chicago department store on the idea of handling it on an exclusive basis. Just as we got going, I discovered that a business associate had made a few changes on the device and was merchandising it himself. That, of course, put an end to the association. I went into business for myself. Now that the Lord had blessed me with the idea for the new rug-cleaning process I didn't want to ruin it by my inexperience. Andrew Carnegie is reported to have said that he wanted his epitaph to read: "Here lies a man who knew how to enlist in his service better men than himself." Facing the same need, I asked God to help me find some, and He soon showed me that He had already put two of them into my life.

I had met one of them on a Sunday evening during the winter of 1942-43. A blizzard had struck the city that day, tying up public transportation. Gas rationing was then in effect, and Lil and I debated all day whether to use our car to drive the considerable distance to our church, and we finally decided against it. Then I remembered noticing a little church nearby; I had observed its announcement of Sunday evening services, so Lil and I went there.

Singing was going on as we entered. There were perhaps a handful of people present, but the young preacher was singing as though he were trying to be heard above a mob. Then he gave us a sermon in which he seemed to be telling us everything he knew, and as I sat there listening for the better part of an hour, I thought that if the fellow preached like this every Sunday he would wear himself out before he was thirty. He was completely earnest, sincerely concerned, vitally interested in what he was saying, he said it well, but he did have a lot to say. After the service, Lil and I went up to introduce ourselves, and I said: "That was quite a sermon."

"Thank you," he said.

And I said: "It made me think of how this hog raiser found a way to keep himself from going broke. When he called the hogs to feed them and only a few showed up, he didn't give them everything he had."

He looked at me, puzzled, but when he saw that I was joking, he got the point and grinned. The following Sunday, Lil wanted to go back to the same church, and the next thing I knew we were all wrapped up in it. The preacher's name was Ken Hansen, fresh out of Wheaton College. He was serving the church as interim pastor, but this didn't prevent him from doing the job wholeheartedly. The neighborhood was building up fast, and every time a moving van pulled in, Ken was over there introducing himself. The church needed a Sunday School and Ken wanted to build it as rapidly as possible. Lil and I were able to be helpful in doing this. Soon we had more children than we could handle. During this time, Ken Hansen and I became well acquainted. I admired him as a person, I respected him as a Christian and I envied his zeal. He never stopped. He was intensely curious about everything, deeply interested in people. I could see that here was a young man who was going places.

He told me one day that though he definitely knew that he was meant to work for God, he wasn't sure it was as a pastor in Chicago. He was drawn more to the missions and to youth work. I suggested to him that if he ever got the feeling that God wanted him to take a place in the business world I would like to talk to him about it. He said: "Fine." And we dropped the subject, going ahead with our other efforts for several months. The time came when the congregation obtained a permanent pastor. Ken's work was completed. He then accepted a position with a Christian foundation which enabled him to apply his talents in the field of developing Christian youth organizations, a work that appealed to him greatly. For over two years I saw very little of Ken, but shortly before his tenure with the foundation was to end, he telephoned me and we got together. He disclosed that he now felt that God wanted him in the marketplace.

"Anything definite lined up?" I asked.

"I've talked to others but nothing definite," he said.

I said: "Well, let me tell you what's been going on around here." I filled him in on the explosion, the commitment, the growth of the business, and what I thought could be attained.

Ken wanted to think about it, to pray about it. A short time later he agreed to come with us, saying: "It sounds challenging. I know I would enjoy working with you."

"Fine," I said. "Here's the way we'll work it. You start to learn the business by going out on production jobs. Then you can move into sales. This experience will equip you for real leadership. After that, you can step in where you're needed most."

Ken was easy to teach. He took instruction and criticism extremely well and advanced rapidly. He had many

97

talents which the Lord had denied me, so between us we had a fine balance and our business grew rapidly. Ken had a real feel for finances, and I was happy to give him plenty of latitude. I told him: "Pay our bills promptly. Give the men the best wages possible. Pay them first. If there's anything left over, you get paid, and if there's anything left over after that, I'll get paid. And do what you can to keep the sheriff away." Ken has been doing this on an enlarged scale ever since.

The second man God put into my life was already in a position to be helpful. From the mothproofing business I had learned that people who buy expensive things are usually more concerned about services which will keep those things in good shape, and I now applied this to cleaning rugs. I realized that the men who would best know who was buying expensive rugs were those who sold them. For this reason, I went to the rug departments of the State Street stores, explaining my services to salesmen, and I'd say, "Now, if you care to recommend my services and give me a chance to do what I say I can, I'll be glad to pay you a commission just as I would pay anybody else. And if you care to give me the names of your customers who bought carpeting here, I'll go out to see them and you will hear from me again." Some of the salesmen were reluctant because they didn't know me, but others took a chance and it worked out well for all concerned. Also, there was a beneficial side effect. When I called on these prospects, I didn't present myself as a representative of the store, of course, but some of the housewives assumed I was and subsequently telephoned the store to express their satisfaction with the job. Because of this, I had quite a few recommendations piled up in the stores when the time came to approach management to set up a program for retailers.

Meanwhile, I had decided to approach the carpet manufacturers for recommendations. I had done this previously to some extent with the mothproofing and had made some good contacts. One of them was Bob Wenger, a Chicago representative of one of the country's biggest rug manufacturers. I liked the man, and the better acquainted I became in the rug industry, the more I heard about his excellence and integrity as an executive. I had several discussions with him about rug cleaning.

Then, in 1946, a downtown hotel was extensively damaged by a fire. I put in a bid for the cleaning and restoration work and was awarded the contract. By coincidence, by the will of God, I know, the insurance company called in Bob Wenger as mediator between the company and the hotel to determine what could be salvaged. Because of this, we worked together closely, and what had been a business relationship became a friendship. He mentioned one day that at the end of the year he was leaving his rug company and going into another area of the industry. As soon as I heard that, I asked him to come to work with me. The invitation surprised him, but he seemed interested and we had a long talk. I explained how I had come to dedicate the company to the Lord, I defined my religious convictions, assured him that I had no trouble mixing religion and business, and that if he did, I had the wrong man. Bob, a Catholic, assured me that he had absolutely the same convictions that I had. Shortly afterward, Bob came out to our plant, met Ken Hansen and the men who were working for us. Ken worked out the incorporation papers, and on January 1, 1947, Wade, Wenger & Associates were in business. Moreover, each of the men who had been with me over the years were given some stock which assured them, if they didn't already know it, that we were all one big family, working for God.

There was a wonderful spirit in the company at every level. Whether a man worked in the front office or out in the shipping room, he knew that his efforts were as important to what we were trying to achieve for the Lord as those of us who were running the place. I guess we all felt like the hod carrier named Pat who had a brother who was a bishop. One day somebody said to Pat: "The talents in your family are certainly unevenly divided." And Pat said: "Yes, my brother couldn't do my job to save his life." People aren't born with that attitude. It is a conviction that grows when a man realizes that whatever the horizon of his job there exists within it an opportunity for excellence. The pursuit of excellence is what broadens both the man and his horizon.

The best example I know of this is Ty Cobb, probably the best ballplayer the game ever produced. His lifetime average in a 24-year career was .367, but he hit over .400 several years. He won twelve batting championships and set many records that have never been surpassed. He was a master at stealing base; one year he stole 96, and his lifetime total was 892. It was said of Cobb that he would be first at the ball park the day after any day he didn't get a hit, even paying someone to throw to him so he could get his timing back. Ty Cobb didn't play ball this way because it was required of him by contract. He did it because he just *had* to. He had a compulsion to do it. His will to win, his determination to do well and then do better equipped him with a boldness that made him a legend in his own time.

This boldness has a place in the business world. It can be the vitality that gives a company its lifeblood. But that blood will run thin unless it is fortified daily with spiritual vitamins, and this is where the Bible comes in as a factor in business. It is something we must keep working at. As Paul wrote the Philippians on the subject of personal perfection necessary for spiritual resurrection: "Not as though I had already attained, either were already perfect: but I follow after, if that I may apprehend that for which also I am apprehended of Christ Jesus. Brethren, I count not myself to have apprehended: But this one thing I do, forgetting those things which are behind and reaching forth unto those things which are before, I press toward the mark for the prize of the high calling of God in Christ Jesus." (Phil. 3:12, 13, 14.)

When God made this planet, it didn't bear much resemblance to the world as we know it today. In my own lifetime I have witnessed revolutions in daily life: the automobile, the airplane, television, atomic energy, frozen foods, indoor plumbing, antibiotics, the list is endless. And yet the basic materials to produce all these things were here from the moment this planet came into being. Selman Waksman, who received the Nobel Prize in 1952 for the development of streptomycin, once said that God has provided us in Nature with the answers to all our ills and that as scientists get to understand Nature better they will be able to produce more medical wonders. In other words, man "creates" nothing; he merely comes to identify what God has created and then ascertains how to use it. At the beginning, God assured Adam and Eve that if they followed His instructions He would make their life a Garden of Eden. We all know how that turned out. But God's assurances of protection and guidance to those who show their love for Him by obeying Him are with us now just as they were then and to receive them we just have to get a better understanding of what He wants of us. He has made that clear in the Bible.

The executive who operates his business only on a short-range basis, who is concerned only with current success, is going to pass from one crisis to the next, until his head is reeling. Success, Webster's dictionary says, is the favorable termination of a venture. The termination of the venture of living is the Judgment of the Lord, and our success there depends on what has happened along the way. Therefore, the executive who has long-range as well as short-range plans will recognize that daily crises are merely the challenges which test the wisdom of what he has planned for the distant future. As long as he is consistent in his judgments, everything will work out, and as long as the basis for his judgments is a source as consistent as the Bible he will work out better than he hoped. There is tremendous peace of mind in the company that knows this and practices it. A businessman's ulcers don't come from the daily crises; they come when he panics as he tries to double-deal his way around the crises. In a company dedicated to the Lord, there can be no double-dealing. In such a company, the only daily crisis is trying to do a better job. This is the pursuit of excellence that the Lord requires of us, as a company and as individuals, and in such a company each individual feels that he is not merely a cog in a machine but a cog without which the machine can't turn. This is when you get both individuality and team spirit in a company. This is when the vitality appears that can make each day hum. There is peace of mind because there is peace of soul.

6

THE BIBLE: THE GUIDE
FOR BUSINESSMEN

In Luke 12, Jesus tells about a farmer who had such a bumper crop one year that he didn't know what to do with it all. Instead of sharing the harvest with the less fortunate farmers, he decided to build bigger barns to store his crop, and he said to himself: "I will say to my soul, 'Soul thou hast much goods laid up for many years; take thine ease, eat, drink and be merry.'" Then God said to him: "Thou fool, this night thy soul shall be required of thee: then whose shall these things be which thou hast provided?"

In telling this parable, Jesus said: "Take heed and beware of covetousness: for a man's life consists not in the abundance of the things which he possesses."

For the businessman, this is one of the most significant passages of the Bible. Naturally, we all want our companies to make a profit. We have an obligation to the stockholders to keep the company in the black. We have a responsibility to our employees to keep the money coming in so they can get paid. But if profits are all we care about, bigger and bigger profits every year, then we run the risk of losing our spiritual perspective. Jesus asked: "What shall it all profit a man if he shall gain the whole world and lose his own soul?"

I've heard of men who admittedly turned their business over to the Lord in the expectation that this was the surest and swiftest road to riches. In effect they were saying: "God is incapable of failure, so now my company should really take off." I wonder how many such men run one of the 15,000 companies that will go out of business this year. The Lord never offered to take over a man's life to such an extent. To each of us He gave a free will, and even the man who has made himself completely dependent on the Lord has to make his own decisions and be responsible for them. But the Lord has provided the basis for right decisions in the Bible and a man can't ask for much more than that.

Often I am asked how to use the Bible for guidance, at least how I use it. There is only one way: to become so familiar with the Bible that thinking in terms of it is part of your nature. The man who has never held a Bible in his hands before would do best to start with the gospels by Matthew, Mark, Luke and John. If he has gone to church at all in his life, he will be somewhat acquainted with what these writers have to say. Even if his knowledge is limited to what he has seen in Bible-based movies or what he reads in newspapers around Easter and Christmas, he will have something to start with. Knowing a little about what he is reading will be important in sustaining his interest during the first few weeks of developing the habit of reading the Bible daily. I've known men who made a snap decision to read the Bible from cover to cover, started with the first chapter of Genesis, then ran into such a confusion of names in the first dozen pages that this was as far as they got.

Reading one chapter a day is advisable. Of course, there are verses in the Bible that can provide a man with enough food for thought for the rest of his life, but the businessman who is seeking a working knowledge of the Bible will be doing well if he can grasp the message that each chapter contains. The message, after all, is what he is after. He wants to know how it applies to him and how he can apply it in his daily life. This is the purpose of reading the Bible, the purpose for which it was intended.

Even at the rate of a chapter a day, a man will have over three years of reading before him, and he will have to do some supplemental reading of Bible commentaries and ancient history if he wants to acquire a clear understanding, particularly of the Old Testament. But it doesn't take long to get to love the Bible, and the man who truly accepts it as the Word of God will do the outside reading not because he has to but because he wants to. And reading isn't enough. You've got to do some thinking. At our house, my wife and I discuss during breakfast what we've read aloud before starting the meal. This has been going on for twenty-five years. We have, of course, read the entire Bible, but we have found it more rewarding to concentrate for as long as necessary on a particular book which we want to understand better, and in this way we move back and forth between the two testaments. Some men tell me private meditation after a morning Bible reading is helpful in assimilating the daily message. Others like the "Bible Breakfast Clubs" which exist in most cities across the country and at which groups of businessmen have the opportunity to discuss Bible passages together while breakfasting once a week in a convenient downtown restaurant.

The process is somewhat like learning a foreign language. To make real progress you must train yourself to think in that language. To make real progress with the Bible, you must train yourself to think in its language as you go through your day making decisions. Don't expect that you'll suddenly become a business genius and every decision will bring in a fortune for the company. In fact if you're really trying to bring the Bible into your life you may have to make a decision that will send the fortune out the window.

Our company had to make a decision of this kind at a time when we were still young and needed every penny we could earn. From the time we had entered the rug-cleaning business, I had felt that it would be good for everybody if stores made our service a regular part of their rug departments. My idea was that a salesman would tell a customer to call the store whenever the rug needed cleaning, the store would notify us and we would go and do the job, with the store getting a percentage. Also, at the time of purchase, we would be notified, add the customer's name to our prospect list and make periodic checks on the condition of the rug, again giving the store a percentage when we did the job. We would also receive records of past sales to check out regularly. To me, this was good for the customer because of the care given the rug, it was good for the store because it enhanced the store's service image, and it was good for us because it brought in business.

It took me over six years to convince a store management that this was a good idea, but it didn't take them long to find out how good an idea it was. In a year we were doing a high volume of business. For obvious reasons, the store didn't inform us that it had obtained a different cleanser and had gone into the on-location cleaning service on its own. As the calls came in, the store took as many jobs as its gradually growing cleaning department could handle, passing the leftovers on to us. This came to our attention when we received a complaint from a customer who wasn't on our list. We did some checking around and discovered what was going on.

Our first reaction was the normal one—we hit the ceiling. Not only was the store violating our agreement, but they were actually doing the cleaning of many jobs which our own salesmen had sold. It was a bad situation and it understandably riled us considerably. Then as Christians we realized we would have to resolve this in a Christian manner if we were to live up to the principles to which the company was dedicated. The Bible told us what to do.

Paul wrote to the Romans: "Recompense to no man evil for evil." Now that is just as plain as a wart on your nose. The Saviour Himself had something to say about this matter of vindictiveness. Luke tells of the day when Jesus and the disciples were on their way to Jerusalem and they came to an unfriendly Samaritan village where they were not permitted to stay for the night. Annoyed, James and John asked: "Lord, shall we command fire to come down from Heaven and consume these people?" Luke says that Jesus turned on them and rebuked them, saying: "You know not what manner of spirit you are of. The Son of man is not come to destroy men's lives but to save them." Clearly, then, as Christians, as followers of Christ, as men who tried to imitate Him in our daily lives, we couldn't be destructive. But we needn't turn the other cheek, either.

So after we cooled off and asked the Lord to forgive us for losing our tempers, we talked the thing over in a Christian way. Nobody had to consult the Bible. We had all studied the Bible and knew what was expected of us. Satan can quote the Bible as well as anyone else, but his trouble is that he doesn't live it, and we were trying to. We didn't want to be in the position of the pastor's wife who was asked by her husband not to spend too much money for a while, particularly on clothes, until he got out of a financial bind that was temporarily gripping him. A few days later she came home with a new dress, and as the pastor was looking at it he said: "It's sure pretty, honey, but I asked you not to buy any clothes for a while, remember?" She said: "Yes, dear, but I was in the store and I saw this lovely dress, and Satan tempted me." He said: "Now, dear, you know the answer to that situation from the Bible. You were just to say, 'Get thee behind me, Satan.'" The woman said: "I did that, dear, but when he got behind me he said it looked beautiful from the back too."

We didn't want Satan anywhere near us. We got in touch with the store management and told them we wouldn't be able to do business with them any more. But rather than leave them in a jam with a backlog of new orders coming in every day as a result of a customer canvass we had made, we said we'd go along with them for six months, which we figured would be enough time for them to expand their rug-cleaning department to the point where they could handle the whole thing themselves. And that's the way we settled it.

The Scriptures are filled with stories of men who returned good for evil and I believe they were meant to serve as examples for us. For instance, in Genesis, the first book of the Bible, we read about Joseph, who was sold into slavery by his jealous brothers. He was badly treated, unjustly jailed for years with no recourse whatever. One day he was suddenly called from prison to interpret a dream that was troubling no less a person than the Pharaoh. Quickly he shaved and changed clothes and was rushed before the king. Joseph revealed that the dream told of impending famine and urged the great one to quickly appoint a wise leader who would supervise all harvesting in the land and store food in preparation for the scarcity that was coming. Pharaoh immediately appointed Joseph governor of Egypt with authority second only to his own. Joseph had been hopelessly imprisoned in the morning—in control of all of Egypt in the afternoon.

Because of the famine that swept through that part of the world, Joseph's family was now having a rough time, and his brothers went into Egypt to try to buy some corn. They didn't recognize Joseph but he recognized them, and when he let them know who he was they feared that his chance had come to even the score. Instead, he forgave them, loaded them with food and money, and told them that if things didn't improve at home they should come back. Joseph is now acknowledged to be one of the great heroes of the Bible. People often emulate their heroes, and this single example of Joseph's goodness, which brought him divine favors, should provide every businessman with something to emulate.

Moses provides a similar example. During the Exodus he led the Hebrews through the part of Arabia where the Midian people lived and he took a Midian woman as his wife. Miriam and Aaron—his sister and brother—

were upset about this because they regarded the woman as a foreigner, and they became critical of him. They began to wonder why God should speak only through Moses, and, talking themselves into believing that He also spoke through them, they tried to pass themselves off as prophets. God saw all this of course, and He summoned the three of them into the tabernacle where, in effect, he said: "When I want a prophet I'll pick a prophet, and I have chosen Moses, not you two, and you know it. How is it then, that you weren't afraid to speak against him?" This was enough to put the fear of the Lord into Miriam. She fell to the ground and her body became like a leper's. Then Aaron got scared. He begged Moses to forgive him and pleaded with him to do something about Miriam. Moses, who recorded this particular event himself, was a mild man who didn't push his weight around. As the leader of the Hebrews he could have shut up Miriam and Aaron himself, but this would have been contrary to his nature. Now the Lord had shown His wrath and punished Miriam for turning against Moses. Had Moses been a different kind of man, he might have accepted this as God's confirmation of his leadership and let it go. Maybe God was giving Moses a chance to prove the kind of man he was. Seeing what had happened and grief stricken by it, Moses cried out: "Heal her now, O God, I beseech Thee!" And God healed her. Thus did God demonstrate Moses' qualifications as a just and forgiving leader by letting him make the decision.

Esther was another who faced decision.

The Bible tells us this orphaned Jewess had been adopted by an older cousin, Mordecai, and these two, along with thousands of other Jews, had been brought under Persian rule. It was during this time that the Persian King, Ahasuerus, sent word to his officers throughout the land to bring in the best-looking candidates from whom he could choose a queen. Now Esther was beautiful and Mordecai thought that if her nationality wasn't known she would stand a chance in any competition. He reasoned that if Esther could move into the palace, she would be in a position to know the king's moods. Since the king's treatment of the Jews seemed to be governed by his moods, her presence might well mean she could keep her people posted on what to expect.

Esther was one of those chosen to go to the palace for the final selection by the king, and off she went with instructions from Mordecai not to reveal her nationality.

She became queen and sent messages to Mordecai who often appeared at the palace gate. One day Mordecai sent word to Esther that he had overheard a plot to kill the king. Esther warned the king, giving credit to Mordecai, and she moved into even greater favor with the king.

As a result of the plot, there was a palace shakeup and a man by the name of Haman was given a top job. Mordecai, who was spending considerable time at the palace gate, angered Haman because, as a Jew, he refused to do the customary bowing to Haman. Instead of dealing with Mordecai individually about the matter, Haman wanted to kill all the Jews in the country. Immediately he told the king that there were people in the provinces living by their own laws, ignoring the king's laws. Haman said he wanted to get rid of these people. The Bible doesn't indicate whether the king knew Haman was talking about the Jews, but he told him to do what he wished about the people. With matters now in his own hands, Haman set a date for excution of the Jews. When Mordecai heard the decree, he sat at the palace gate in mourning clothes and cried.

Esther, unaware of the decree, was baffled when word got to her of Mordecai's actions, and she sent him new clothes. He refused the clothes, but sent with the servant a copy of Haman's execution decree and a plea that she go before the king on behalf of her people.

This put Esther in a spot. Anyone who went before the king without being summoned risked death. She reasoned that since he had not asked to see her for thirty days he would not be in a receptive mood, and that could mean the end for her.

But even this excuse wasn't enough for Mordecai. He sent back word that she shouldn't think that just because she was in the king's palace she would escape execution any more than the other Jews. His closing words were: "Who knows whether you have not come to the kingdom for such a time as this?"

Esther knew he was right. No excuse, no matter how

legitimate, could cover up what she had to do. She sent word of her decision to Mordecai, asking him and all the Jews to pray for her, and with determination said: "I will go to the king . . . and if I perish, I perish."

As it turned out, the king did receive her and as a result the Jewish people were saved from death. Mordecai even became the king's righthand man. The events which followed Esther's decision provide exciting reading, and even more, they show how the Lord honored Esther's decision and answered the prayers of her people. Esther's courage should inspire any executive who is hesitant about paying the price for doing the right thing.

The situation we faced in dealing with the store which broke its agreement was an instance when a working knowledge of the Bible gave us guidance. An aspect of each of these Bible stories convinced us of what we had to do if we really wanted to honor the Lord and if we wanted Him to honor us.

As angry men we could have cut off our services to the store immediately, leaving them with a pile of orders and many complaining customers. I will concede we thought about doing that while we were angry.

But Joseph didn't cut off his hungry brothers when he was in a position to give them food.

The store men had pulled something behind our backs and we could easily have rationalized that they deserved to be left with any consequences.

Miriam and Aaron had been underhanded and God had to deal with them, but Moses, instead of sitting back and enjoying their predicament, cried to God on their behalf, and God approved his decision. In business, our decisions may not involve such extreme circumstances, but they do involve such extreme responsibility.

And finally, at the time we were faced with our business decision, we needed money and assurance of the store's business. We might have pretended that we hadn't learned what the store was doing and gone along with them for a year or two as we eased our financial situation and the store built up its rug-cleaning department, but this would have been condoning evil.

Esther, too, could have pretended not to know about the decree to kill the Jews, but she recognized silence was wrong and did what was right regardless of the risk. Esther's words: "If I perish, I perish" were ours too, as far as the business was concerned. We all knew this. But knowing what God wanted us to do, we made the transition promptly and were better men for doing it. It was not strange to us that as we did less and less business with the store we were doing more and more business on our own. We finished that year better than any before it.

7

THE COMPETITION IS YOU

In 1954 I went through a period when I wasn't feeling too well and my doctor suggested a thorough examination. After numerous tests, we sat down in his office
and from the look on his face I knew it was serious. He
said he considered me a mature man who could take the
truth, and he felt I should know it. I had atherosclerosis,
a hardening of the lining of the arteries, and I had it
bad. enough that it was advisable for me not to make
any long-range plans. I assured the doctor I was not afraid
of death, that I knew where I was going, that my hope
was in Christ, and though I wasn't looking forward to
death I knew it was on the way and I had already put
the matter entirely in the Lord's hands. With that out
of the way, we discussed what I would have to do to be
able to remain alive. He gave me some good advice on
rest and diet. He was particularly concerned about anx-
ieties in my life and was surprised to hear me say that I

didn't have any. He thought this was unusual for a businessman.

Perhaps it was, but not for me. In the first place, I had men capable of running the business better than I could run it myself. I had, of course, helped train these men, but they had their own God-given talents which they were using excellently. Also, in addition to the stock we gave the men when the company was incorporated, they were able to buy more whenever they wished, thus becoming active owners in the company they worked for. Moreover, we had begun our system of granting franchises to men in other cities; men who, though they used our equipment and products, were actually in business for themselves. Therefore, though I habitually referred to the organization as "my company," this was more out of affection than possession, for the company was partially owned by practically everybody who worked for it, and ultimately it was owned by the Lord. We all knew that and acknowledged it daily.

The acknowledgment, in fact, led to the name by which the company became known. We had to admit that "Wade, Wenger and Associates" was quite a mouthful for the switchboard operator when we grew big enough to have one. More than that, we wanted a generic name which the franchise holders could use, and we wanted it to be a name which could be applied to the diversified services we were taking on and at the same time indicate the basic philosophy of the company. The name we chose almost evolved by itself. As a company, we were in the business of on-location cleaning and maintenance services. As individuals and as a company, we were working for the Lord—we were servants of the Master. The word "ServiceMaster" struck us all as perfect in every area. When a man is working with a company of men to whom serving the Master is a way of life, the only anxiety he may have is whether he is serving enough. Everything else seems to be taken care of.

Even so, being told that you are closer to death than you thought you were produces a state of shock. That evening, my wife and I had a dinner date at a country club, and I didn't feel much like talking as we drove out there. Lil knew about the medical examination, of course, and knew I had been told the results, and I knew she had been waiting to be told. Thinking it over, I had realized that it was as important for her to know the truth as it was for me, but I wanted a more propitious moment for it. I waited until we were seated at our table and had ordered and then, my own gloom somewhat dispelled by the pleasant atmosphere, I told her what the doctor had said. She was very much concerned.

I took out the Bible I usually carry with me and suggested: "Now, let's take a look in the Scriptures." We often made our devotions a part of our meal, so there was nothing unusual in this. I had no special passage in mind but I knew from experience that the Psalms invariably had something helpful at moments when I might be feeling low, and as I paged through them my eye caught some verses in Psalm 118. I had read them many times before, but tonight they held a distinct promise. I read to Lil:

"The Lord is my strength and song, and is become my salvation. The voice of rejoicing and salvation is in the tabernacles of the righteous: the right hand of the Lord doeth valiantly . . . I shall not die, but live, and declare the works of the Lord. The Lord has chastened me sore: but He hath not given me over unto death."

Nothing could have been more apt. Nothing could have been more helpful. Lil and I both knew that the Lord had spoken to us again. We remained silent, in prayer, for a few moments. Then we relaxed and became aware again of our surroundings, a roomful of happy people, many of them fresh off the golf course. Lil knew I enjoyed the game, and she asked: "Did the doctor say you can continue to play golf?"

We had discussed golf. I told Lil: "He was against it at first because many men get so tense about the game. But after I explained how I felt about golf he said it would be okay."

The tensions which grow out of the competition between men playing golf together would take all the fun out of the game for me. When I play golf, my only interest is in shooting par, breaking it if I can. If the fellow I'm playing with birdies every hole I may envy him but I'm not going to resent him. I'm not going to ruin my game by trying to beat his. He isn't my competition, he's a friend I'm playing golf with. My competition is the course. When the course was laid out, some genius figured out how many strokes a good golfer would require to get from each tee to each cup, and my job is to match it. Some days I beat the course; when the course starts winning too often, I go see the pro to find out what I'm doing wrong. When I win often enough, the fellows with me can be sure of a free lunch. The idea, then, of becoming contentious toward friends who are merely trying to do the same thing I am would be the fastest way to wreck both the game and the friendships.

There is, for that matter, no room for contention even in the world of business competition. The businessman who spends his time worrying about the fellow down the street is merely taking that much time away from his own company, time that could be invested in improving his own products and services to the point where the competition couldn't compete with him. Moreover, the Christian businessman has a Bible-prescribed obligation to keep contention out of his effort to surpass his competition. "Let nothing be done in strife," Paul wrote the Philippians, "or vainglory, but in lowliness of mind let each esteem others better than themselves."

In business, a man must believe that his product or service is the best he can make it or he cannot operate in good faith. Quality, then, should be the basis of business competition, but anybody in business knows that this is not always the case. Unfair competition abounds at every level of business, even within the same company, and the Christian businessman is obligated to take a stand against it even if it means he perishes. The psalmist said: "Many are my persecutors and mine enemies, yet do I not decline from Thy testimonies." In other words, the boys are giving me a rough time, Lord, but I'm trusting You and the Bible because that's the way I know it must be.

The Lord Himself gave instructions in this regard when, in Matthew 10:16, He said: "Behold, I send you forth as sheep in the midst of wolves: be ye therefore wise as serpents, and harmless as doves." Every businessman likes to think of himself as being wise, but remaining dovelike when you're surrounded by a pack of snarling wolves demands all the staying power a man's faith has. And yet we are told that we must. Several years ago, we at ServiceMaster found out how fast the wolves can come close to turning the doves into a few leftover feathers in a mighty short time.

We were doing the on-location rug cleaning for a number of retail stores and progressing well. Then a store we considered highly reputable got in touch with us with a proposition. They pointed out that most people were still sending their rugs out to be cleaned, which we knew. Then they said: "We're certainly satisfied with the on-location work you are doing for our customers. But we want to make a single package of our rug-cleaning services, giving all the work to one company.

This will be much simpler for us. So if you people will start a rug-cleaning plant we'll give you the package."

Up to this point, having a big plant of our own was not in our plans. We felt that doing our work on other premises saved us from a sizable overhead. But this offer tempted us. It would definitely secure our position with the store. Other companies had now gone into on-location work and were scrounging for contracts. By going along with the deal we would, we believed, keep this important store on our list. Also, the Korean War was then brewing. We knew that if it boiled over many of our personnel would be recalled to military duty and we would not have enough men to do the on-location work. We began to give the offer serious thought.

We looked for a factory building and found one. Ken Hansen inspected both it and our finances and established that we would need about $25,000 to put the building into usable condition. I had an idea that I knew where to get it.

A short time before, my wife and I had decided we needed a bigger house for our growing children and we put the one we had up for sale. A lot of people came around and looked the house over, and then the dickering would start. I lost a lot of time and patience with this, as people tried to bargain with me. When another man came to the door for an inspection I told him: "Now, listen. I will show you the house from top to bottom. I will point out everything that's good about the place and everything that's bad. Then I will tell you what I believe the house is worth, and I'm telling you now that I won't ask a penny more or take a penny less than that. So there will be no dickering."

We went through the house. Then I told the man how much I wanted and he agreed to it and he said: "I've enjoyed doing business with you. I've never met a man before who was so forthright. If you ever run into a business transaction where you need an investor, let me know."

I needed one now. I telephoned this man, explained that my company had an opportunity for expansion and we needed some working capital. I had $25,000 in stock for sale, I told him, and I asked if he were interested in any of it. He said that he had about $6,000 in cash on hand and would be right over with it. I thanked him, and when I told the fellows what had happened we were all sure this was God's way of letting us know that we were on the right track. It didn't occur to any of us that our customary long-range view had become very short in a hurry. In a minute, this man called back and told me that he had some relatives downstate who might be interested in picking up the remaining stock. Would I drive there with him to talk it over? I would. Two days later, I had the $25,000. Who could ask for a clearer go-ahead?

The money was used for alterations in the building we had leased, knocking out walls, moving stone partitions. While this was going on, we were trying to operate, sometimes with a side of the building wide open. I can recall Ken sleeping on a pile of Oriental rugs to protect them through the night. We were under that kind of pressure. And then the project backfired.

First, we had banked on the department store to send us enough business to cover most of the operating costs while we went out after other customers. Checking the industry, we learned that the store wasn't doing anywhere near the business they had promised and had very little chance of ever approaching the figure they had quoted. Why they made the package offer was something we never solved. But having gone this far, we considered going ahead on our own. However, the Korean War broke out, the War Production Board stopped the manufacture of equipment we desperately needed, and no one could predict when the material would become available again. We were considerably shaken. There we were, stuck with a plant that was much larger than we needed, and all because we had been romanced by a dealer who had promised more than he could produce. And he had known it all along.

The dog-eat-dog philosophy of business has become so generally accepted that people are more surprised by the exception to the rule than by the rule itself. Businessmen squirm as more and more government controls are imposed on industry if only to assure the little guy some degree of fair play, but if we were all fair we wouldn't need the controls. We have police in our communities because there are certain people who prefer stealing to get what they want to working for it. Government policing becomes necessary in business not because of the rampant dishonesty and deception but rather because of the popular attitude that anything goes. Understandably, businessmen resent the interference. This is, after all, supposed to be a country of free enterprise. The trouble begins, however, when the enterprise starts getting too free and easy. If we want to keep government out of business, then business will have to do its own policing, with the government meanwhile policing itself as well. In each instance, the man to do the job is the man who is managing the team.

The test of a good baseball team manager is not only producing a winning team but knowing exactly which man to choose as a pinch hitter when things are all tied up in the last of the ninth. World Series have been won by managers who knew their players that well. A good business manager also knows what each of his men can do, as he knows the right man to send to bat in a challenging situation. If he is a Christian, he knows, too, that in addition to government agencies which serve as umpires the deal is also being observed by the Lord, so the game is played by the rules not only to avoid penalties but so that it will be pleasing unto the Lord. Every man in the company should be imbued with this same attitude, which is how the manager puts together a trained and coordinated team. Give such men a product that meets the competition and you've got yourself a pennant that can be won without having to put stones in the other team's shoes.

Paul warned the Galatians: "If ye bite and devour one another, take heed that ye be not consumed one of another." This is an apt warning to businessmen who think competition is reason for cannibalism in the marketplace. Doctors say it's bad for your health to eat and run. It's equally bad for your business if you think you can take time out to devour your competition when your main concern should be keeping your company moving ahead. When the front runner in a track meet glances over his shoulder he isn't thinking of tripping anyone. He just wants to know how much more steam he's going to have to put up to stay out there by himself.

I view business competition in the same light. I regard competition not as a threat but a challenge. Rather than worry about how much business other companies are getting, I am concerned with improving our own standards at ServiceMaster so that more people will want to do business with us. God gives to every man the power to be not just better than the other guy but better than he himself ever thought he could be. The real spirit of competition, then, should be in fulfilling one's own potentials, not in thwarting somebody else's. We should compete with ourselves, never being satisfied, progressing from what we are to what we ought to be, then going on to all that we can be.

Paul also told the Galatians: "Let every man prove his own work, and then shall he have rejoicing alone and not in another. For every man shall bear his own burden." The burden is the responsibility—the duty—to do his job. Once a man learns to bear his burden he finds that he can help others bear theirs, and the Bible goes further by saying that actually we should bear each other's burden, help each other do our jobs. In terms of competition, this sometimes has stimulating results. The man who builds a better mouse trap, for example, is really lifting the standards of the mouse-trap industry because everybody else in it will have to make improvements if he wants to hold his ground, and so the situation is improved for everybody except the mice.

The morale within a company is a basic factor in the firm's conduct toward competitors. I know of some companies that operate on a contest basis, pitting the various departments against each other, with cash bonuses or time off as rewards. This is child psychology and has no place in the business world that is supposed to be populated by mature men and women. An employee is hired at a specific salary to do a specific job, and as the company prospers so does he, but if he is willing to work a little harder only when he is baited by bonuses he really isn't doing his job in the first place. The boss who thinks that putting his men into competition with each other will get more work out of them is actually creating dissension within his own ranks. Some men have told me that there was so much competition in their company that they never knew whether their name would still be on the door when they showed up for work in the morning. When a man has to fight the fellow across the hall in order to keep his job he's not going to worry much about ethics when it comes to fighting the competitor across the street to make the sale. It shouldn't be surprising that the companies which have the most vicious reputations in business competition also have the biggest staff turnovers.

No matter how big a company is, it is a single unit, and each employee has his own identity with the finished product. The Bible says: "As the body is one and has many members, and all the members of the body, many as they are, form one body, so also is it with Christ." The passage goes on to say that though we are all individuals, with different talents, different gifts of the Holy Spirit, some seemingly more important than others, we are all of equal value as members of the Christian body, the mystical body of Christ, just as the foot is as important as the hand and the ear is as important as the eye in the human body, each part performing the function for which the Lord created it. In a company dedicated to the Lord every employee can have this same feeling of vital membership, and it is more than attitude. It is a fact.

We at ServiceMaster are very much aware of this fact.

··· 8 ···

TRUTH IN THE
MARKETPLACE

When I am interviewing a man who is seeking a position with our company, it is my policy to question him about his personal habits, including the use of alcohol and tobacco. My concern about smoking and drinking is not a matter of morality but a matter of self-discipline. Paul warned the early Christians of the dangers in letting a personal habit become their master. It could take over their lives. Whatever else they are, smoking and drinking are habits to which the users can become addicted, needing more of them every day, until they are enslaved. Whether a person smokes or drinks, or both, is immaterial to me personally and doesn't affect my feelings toward him as an individual. But it is the idea of the habit that I dislike and distrust. I wouldn't risk having a man working for me who had so completely lost his freedom of choice that he couldn't say no to a personal habit. I would have my doubts about his ability to discipline himself along more important lines.

Moreover, our business is service. Dependability is the essence of service. Many of our customers come to us through retailers who have worked years to build a reputation for integrity and dependability, and our company becomes responsible for that reputation as well as our own when we take a job. In view of our stewardship to these people, I simply cannot take a chance on a man who admits he is a victim of his habits. When I sent my first boys out on service jobs, I immediately received fine comments on them as craftsmen and gentlemen from both the customer and the store. To be sure, we have since made a couple of mistakes, and with such disastrous consequences that I now consider it my prerogative and my duty to learn as much as I can about a man before sending him out to represent a company that is dedicated to the Lord.

When I was playing ball I chewed tobacco for a while. We all did, which was probably the reason I took it up. The moist wad was supposed to absorb the bushel of dust we'd eat in the course of a game but I think it had something to do with nerves too. I know that the worse a game was going for us the harder we'd all chomp on the stuff. But at best it was a filthy habit and I soon gave it up. It's understandable that a man's nerves should get jumpy when he's under pressure whether he's playing ball or doing business, but there's nothing in tobacco that's going to help him. The scientists back me up on this, based on the conflicting reports on why people smoke. Some smokers say that a cigarette soothes them and others say that it sparks them. If the same brand can have such opposite effects on two people, then the emotional factor is not in the cigarette but in the smoker's mind, and he's kidding himself. It's bad enough to have the habit but it's worse not to understand it, and the man who doesn't understand his habits isn't going to be very dependable in a pinch of any kind.

The habit of needing a couple of drinks before facing pressure is even more indicative of insecurity. Alcohol makes people drunk, unaware of the situation around them, and the man who needs a couple of drinks is telling me that he wants to be only moderately drunk, moderately unaware, moderately unafraid of the responsibilities facing him and the decisions he must make. I wouldn't get into a car with a driver in that shape. I wouldn't let him represent me in any business deal, either.

When I am under pressure I pray, and I don't care where I am or what others may think of it. The Psalms assure: "Be still, and know that I am God: I will be exalted among the heathen, I will be exalted in the earth. The Lord of hosts is with us: the God of Jacob is our refuge." That is both soothing and sparkling enough for me. I believe that prayer, even a private prayer, can keep us calm, alert and trustful in the Lord in any business situation, particularly when self-discipline is the factor that determines the outcome.

It has been my observation that a man who has committed his life to the Lord develops the self-discipline that can make him a winner in any contest. The Lord's rules cover every aspect of life, so a man has to work at it every minute if he expects to live up to his commitment. But this is the only way you get to master anything, especially yourself.

Branch Rickey, the baseball genius, tells a story that illustrates this fact in a very unusual way. There is nothing like it in the record books anywhere. Many years ago when he was managing the St. Louis Browns in a game against Detroit, Detroit came to bat in the last half of the eleventh inning of a tie game. Soon two men were out and there was nobody on base, when up to the plate stepped Ty Cobb. Knowing what kind of hitter Cobb was, Rickey decided it would be safer to walk him to get somebody not so threatening, and he sent the signal out to the pitcher. Cobb got his base on balls and he turned it into the winning run before another ball was pitched. By sheer boldness and skill he forced two wild throws by St. Louis infielders. His daring at first base, his skillful turn at second, his characteristic slide ten feet before he reached third, his quick coordination after the slide all brought about four breaks in his favor. He made what amounted to a home run out of a base on balls.

In the same game, there was a player on the Browns team named Walker who had the physical qualities to be a great player. During the game, he hit what should have been a home run but he was thrown out at third. His slow start to first as he watched the ball sail safely between left and center cost him 20 feet. Next he lost 30 feet in too wide a turn at second. Then seeing the ball apparently on its way to the fence, he slowed down, this cost him another 50 feet. So by now he was 100 feet behind schedule. Suddenly the ball struck an object of some kind on the wall and bounced back into the hands of the surprised centerfielder, who turned and threw a strike into third base. Walker, seeing that a play was being made on him, put on a real burst of speed. He made a great fall-away slide, but right into the ball held by the third-baseman.

Cobb and Walker were the same age, same height, same weight and same speed, but Walker had a better arm and more power at bat. Yet Cobb rose to enduring fame while Walker disappeared into obscurity. Why? Branch Rickey says the difference between the two men was this: Ty Cobb wanted to excel at baseball so badly that he disciplined himself hour after hour, day after day, to perfect the qualities he needed to succeed. Walker punched the clock.

Every once in a while a young fellow comes along in the business world who seems to possess the Ty Cobb attitudes, and the front office gets excited. But after a couple of years he peters out and you wonder why.

Maybe he even becomes the company's "white ele-phant," and there is the problem of what to do with him. My own experiences with a few of these fellows leads me to believe that their shortcoming is that they have set their affections on things here below instead of on the treasures of the Kingdom. Loyalty to the com-pany is a good thing; so is pride in the product, but these are attachments to man-made things. Anything that is man-made isn't going to last long and neither is anything attached to it.

It is only when a man has the high purpose of living for the Lord that he remains constant as an individual who is constantly growing. As ServiceMaster continued to grow, I was always on the lookout for young fellows like that. I wanted men who would not only have the Ty Cobb attitude toward the company but toward all of life. They would, after all, be going into private homes either to sell ServiceMaster to housewives or to do the job, and I wanted these to be the only inten-tions they had in mind. Also, they would sometimes be working alone in a home or an office, and I didn't want to turn any souvenir collectors or snoopers loose in such situations. And some of them would be representing ServiceMaster in negotiations with other companies. The way they conducted themselves would determine whether we were living up to our name or not. Of course, I can't read minds, so when it comes to judging a man I can be taken for a ride as quickly as the next fellow. But this is the reason why, before I hire a man, I try to find out how relevant his religion is to his daily habits in his business.

No employer ever finds enough of the right men. A suggestion of Ken Hansen's, however, did lead to a promising source. We placed an ad in the alumni association publication of his school, Wheaton College, saying: "If you feel God is calling you in business, get in touch with Marion Wade." Evidently the school was still doing a good job. Some fine young men came around to see us and some of them are still here as executives. Also, we found that there were men who were looking for our kind of company to work for. On one occasion, we had decided to award a franchise in a Midwest city, and among those who made inquiries were some people already in the on-location cleaning service but with another company. We went out to talk to them. We had dinner together and visited them in their homes. At bedtime I tucked a couple of little girls in and told them a few Bible stories, and when I returned to Chicago I sent them some Bible-story books which I understand they still have. Shortly afterward, these people decided to come with us. Their former associates tried to get them back. In the course of trying, they learned about the Bible stories and the books, and they said: "How can you beat an outfit like that? They've got the Bible going for them." The truth was the opposite: we were going for the Bible.

The man who looks on his job as his personal ministry in the service of the Lord brings to his work the fullness that God wants it to have. The attitude that the spiritual and the secular worlds cannot be one and the same is shortsightedness in the sacrament of living. A thing becomes secular when you cut God out of it. The man who cuts God out of his business has admitted to the world, even if he doesn't admit it to himself, that he's up to something he'd rather not have God see. The Christian businessman knows that God sees everything and so he conducts himself and his business accordingly.

The prophet Micah puts it on the line when he says: "What does the Lord require of thee, but to do justly, and to love mercy, and to walk humbly with thy God?" Through Micah, the Lord asks: "Shall I count them pure, with the wicked balances, and with the bag of deceitful weights?" If any Bible question is aimed directly at businessmen, that one certainly is. In Leviticus, the Lord is more explicit in saying: "Ye shall do not unrighteousness in judgment, in meteyard, in weight, or in measures. Just balances, just weights, a just ephah [bushel], and a just hin [pint], shall ye have: I am the Lord your God, which brought you out of the land of Egypt. Therefore shall ye observe all my statutes, and all my judgments, and do them: I am the Lord." Like any boss who has to put his foot down once in a while, the Lord, in this passage from Leviticus, puts down His. The Christian businessman will get the point and do what he is told.

What we are told is not very difficult for the man who is more concerned with saving his soul than saving his business. We are told to be honest. In modern terms, this means being honest in our advertising, on our labels, with our prices, with our product and in our dealings. If anybody thinks the business world is living up to this obligation, let him take a look at the numerous government agencies in Washington that have been set up to keep us all in line.

A Christian businessman doesn't need those agencies. He needs only his belief in God and his acceptance of the Bible. Having these, he is aware that his relationship with God and his relationship with his fellowmen are an infallible measure of his stature. He realizes that it's possible to cheat people and get away with it but he knows he can't cheat God. Therefore, unless he is a fool or a hypocrite, he recognizes that just weights and measures are a moral obligation as incumbent upon him as fidelity to his wife. And if he is the boss he sees to it that every man on his staff is equally aware of this responsibility. As the boss, he must be ready to take the blame should anybody working for him get tricky in this regard.

Ever since I went into selling I've encountered people who tried to get a thumb on the scale in one way or another, and many of them ended up like the butcher who had the same habit. A woman entered his shop late one Saturday afternoon and asked for a chicken. Only one remained in the barrel at the end of the busy day. The butcher put it on the scale and told the woman it would cost her $1.85. She asked: "Oh, don't you have a bigger one?" The butcher put the chicken back into the barrel, rattled it around a bit, then brought it up and placed it on the scale again, putting his thumb there as well, and he said: "Well, yes, this is larger. It's $3." The woman said: "Fine. I'll take them both."

While selling insurance, I met a number of prospects who told me they had a friend who wrote their insurance, then gave them half of his first year's commission —they were looking for kickbacks. Later I met a few department store rug buyers who felt they had something extra coming because they set up the appointment at which I persuaded the store management to take on our services. With one such buyer, I said: "Well, okay, if you think you've got it coming, but let's talk to the store president first and see if it's okay with him." He told me to forget it, as I knew he would. But I'll never know how such a man can live with himself under the eyes of God. When Jesus said that a workman is worthy of his meat He didn't say anything about any gravy on the side. I realize that the payola examples I've cited involved small amounts of money, but this is not the point. Dishonesty is dishonesty, no matter when or where it occurs or on whose part. Honesty is not relative; it is absolute.

The offense is greater when it is committed by men in positions of responsibility. The Apostle Paul said: "It is required in stewards that a man be found faithful." That means that God expects us to obey His laws, He requires it. And this applies not only to Christians but to every human being regardless of his religion and even to those who claim to have none. Every man has a conscience, and though men may differ in their theologies the instincts put into them by natural law bind them together on the questions of right and wrong. An atheist knows when he has sinned just as clearly as a struggling Christian. The difference between them is that the Christian, loving God, will repent, while the atheist, loving only himself, will repent only if he gets caught. Caught or not, every man is accountable for his use of the talents God has given him, and the more talents he has the more accountable he is because God requires more of him.

At ServiceMaster, we have learned that a man becomes more sensitive to his accountability to God when we give him the opportunity for more responsibility to the company. We make our plans and set policy at staff conferences, then each man goes back to his office to do his job, using his own brains and his own skills to make his own decisions. When a shortstop sees a fast line drive coming at him like a bullet he doesn't glance over at the manager to find out what he should do. In business a man at the executive level should be able to make his decisions without having to run to the front office every time.

Occasionally I meet employers who don't feel that way. They can hardly bring themselves to delegate authority to a subordinate because of the risk that the fellow might make a mistake. Anybody can make a mistake. Solomon, supposedly the wisest man of his time, made a lot of mistakes—he had a thousand wives. We learn from our mistakes; we grow by them. In my opinion, the essential point in the delegation of authority is that though it presents the chance to fail it also gives a man a chance to exercise his ingenuity and judgment so that he does not fail. Without this risk, there can be no growth, whether to the individual or the company, and there is no such thing as delegation without risk. If authority is not truly delegated to a subordinate, if he is not made responsible for success or failure, he will wither. Unless every man is made to realize that he is his own prime mover, the company's efforts will go down the drain.

It has been my experience that people learn to manage by managing. This is the way ServiceMaster has been built, and we know that the future of our company depends greatly on the manner and the extent to which we continue to delegate authority to the young men who are rising in the firm. As they grow, we grow. The reluctant employer who doesn't recognize this basic axiom is failing in his own stewardship because as boss his personal worth to the business will be judged largely on the basis of his ability to help people grow.

We've made mistakes, of course, occasionally with franchise holders. These men usually start out with tremendous enthusiasm, but we can never tell how long it is going to last. If the man has dedicated his life to the Lord we know we have a better chance for a winner.

We do all we can to help our franchise holders get on their feet, but each man is going to have to work long hours at hard labor for a few years, and if he has nothing to keep him going except personal ambition he is going to wear out before long. For this reason I always explain the ServiceMaster philosophy to a franchise applicant at the outset, assuring that the Lord has been our strength and can be his. Sometimes this is taken with surprise, even embarrassement, and I'm always gratified when a fellow like this writes me several months later and says he has found out the truth of it for himself.

But sometimes we get a daydreamer who thinks that going into business for himself means he can sit back and give orders instead of going out and getting a few. Other times, we've had men who lacked enough commitment to make the self-sacrifices necessary in starting a business. One fellow might be lazy, another might have chosen the wrong product, another simply didn't have the aptitude to run a business, but naturally we couldn't foresee any of these things. We've had a few men who failed because their wives weren't 100 percent behind them, and this can be very serious. I like to meet a man's wife before the contracts are signed so I can explain to her that she's about to go through what my own wife went through many years ago. A man in business for himself can't always choose his own working hours, and if his wife is the type to whom having dinner on time every night is a matter of life or death there is going to be trouble. A good wife tries to make herself part of her husband's business. After all, he most likely went into it for her sake more than his own, so he could provide her and the kids with a better life. Maybe she can cover his telephone until he can afford a secretary; maybe she can handle his books until he is ready for an accountant, but if she does nothing else she can at least be at his side, praying for him every step of the difficult way. Evidently not all wives are like that. We lost one good man because his wife felt the rug-cleaning business wasn't dignified enough for him. This was false pride, and the truth was that the rug-cleaning business wasn't dignified enough for *her*. The Bible warns us that pride goeth before a fall and that before honor comes humility. This poor fellow fell, losing a bit on his investment in the business and returning to a job he had never really liked. But now he had dignity.

A job has only as much dignity as the man gives it, and the best way to dignify a job is to dedicate your efforts to the glory of God. Doing this, a man whose job is spreading manure on a farm field can look at the world with the same dignified self-respect as the President of the United States. There is, these days, too much evaluating of people and things by what meets the eyes, and this is the kind of materialism that is going to put the skids under all of us if we don't return to the true values of our religion and our country.

Not long ago, Ken Hansen had an experience along these lines. One of his sons was working his way through college by doing cleaning jobs for the company during his vacations. One day we got a call from the school for a rush job in one of the buildings, and the boy went over to do it. The job was bigger than we expected, so Ken donned a ServiceMaster coverall and volunteered to help his son in order to meet the deadline. As they were working, one of the boy's professors happened to come into the room, and the youngster paused to introduce his father to the man. As they shook hands, the professor's eyebrows went up and he asked: "Oh? Are you in the rug-cleaning business?" Ken said he was. Then the professor glanced at the boy with an expression that clearly said: "I didn't know your father was a common laborer." Ken read the expression, then shrugged it off. When he got back to the office and told me about it, we shared a sad smile. Ken is in the rug-cleaning business, all right—he is president of a company doing a multimillion-dollar business. I had a similar experience when I was just starting out. A man I knew from the cookware business came out to see me while I was working on a job, and he offered me a position as director of sales training with his company. As I listened, I remained on my hands and knees, working on a rug. Then I thanked him and said no, explaining that I had just gone into business for myself, believed I had a good thing going and preferred to stay where I was. He said: "Marion, why are you groveling around in all that dirt when you could be making many times more than whatever you're earning now and have a job with some dignity besides?" I know he meant well, so I let that pass. Anyway, by staying where I was the Lord was able to lead me where I am.

Appearances, then, can be deceiving, and this works both ways. We've had fellows with us who didn't smoke and didn't drink, but they didn't do much work either. If we discovered this early enough, there wasn't much of a problem, but usually these things don't become noticeable until the man has been around for a while and perhaps even made his way into a position of some importance, on the basis of what appeared to be his potential. Then it becomes obvious that, if the man is doing anything, he is not doing it right, and the company discovers it has a white elephant on its hands. The term "white elephant" is derived, I'm told, from a custom of the kings of Siam some centuries ago. Albino elephants were so rare in the country that each one born became the property of the king and was not allowed to work. Whenever a king got mad at any of his subjects, he would give the man a white elephant, and it wasn't long before the huge, voracious animal ate the man out of house and home.

In business, white elephants present a sticky problem which is always difficult to handle. Usually such a man has been around long enough to become entrenched in a job he has shown he can't do. He has simply stopped growing, he isn't earning his keep, and he is standing in the way of younger, more capable men who are overdue for promotion. The worst part is that often the white elephant hasn't any idea of what's happened. He has, he feels, done his job, and he isn't aware that there have been no results. Finally the moment comes when the situation can't go on any longer, and it's up to the boss to put the cards on the table. I discussed this problem with many employers and we've all agreed that we'd rather be horsewhipped than go through it. If the white elephant had the humility to face facts, to step aside and take a lesser job, the problem would be simpler. It might be simpler but it would never be easy. To tell a man that he has not made the grade is just about the worst thing you can do to him. Rarely will he take a lesser job, rarely will he step back or step aside, and if he won't resign you've got to fire him. The most painful part is that usually he's a man you've grown to like, and you hate yourself for what you feel must be done, and done by you.

Biblically, it is, pure and simple, a matter of the just weights and measures which Christians should both give and expect in their dealings. However innocent the white elephant may be in his heart and mind, the fact remains that the net result is the same as though he had his thumb on the scale. The stockholders, the company, the co-workers, perhaps even the customers, are not getting their money's worth out of the man.

There can be no more excruciating experience for an employer than to have to take action with a white elephant. The employer can only pray that the man has the maturity to discuss the situation calmly and intelligently, and if there can be no resolution within the company perhaps the employer can help the man find a job elsewhere, commensurate to his experience and ability. They may even remain friends. But if the man fails to appreciate that the employer, like himself, is accountable for his stewardship to the company and, more important, to God, then there is no escaping a bleak and bitter confrontation. The Lord did not promise us an easy road. He merely promised to help us over the rough parts.

We in business must press on in our ministry, taking the bitter with the sweet, never knowing how much of either the Lord has put in our paths to test us as we hopefully proceed to the goal of His Heaven and the prize of Himself.

≈ ≈ ≈ 9 ≈ ≈ ≈

DIFFERENCES CAN
PROMOTE GROWTH

Sometimes when I find myself in a situation involving a conflict of opinions, I think about the Quaker farmer who was having more than his usual troubles with his stubborn mule, so he said to it: "Thou knowest I am a Quaker. Thou knowest I can't curse thee, I can't whip thee. What thou dost not know is that I can sell thee to my neighbor down the road and he can beat the living daylights out of thee." It is a fact of business life that conflicts of opinion are going to arise among people on the staff on how a thing should be done or whether it should be done at all, and sometimes when nobody will give an inch I feel like sending for that farmer down the road.

Benefiting from the opinions of others is one of the main reasons for having staff conferences, but the benefits go out the window if there is somebody at the table who is merely being opinionated. The man who is unmovable in an exchange of opinions is usually the man who doesn't have many opinions to move around. It's like the two bums who were trying to get some sleep in the railroad station of a small country-town and the stationmaster gave them a rough time as he threw them out. Then one bum said to the other: "Have you noticed that the smaller the station, the bigger the stationmaster?"

The dedicated Christian knows that the only opinion that counts is the Lord's, and he knows that the Lord's opinions on every possible subject are expressed in the Bible, from the first page to the last. And not only are there opinions on the conflict of opinions but also on the conflicts themselves. Probably the most dramatic example was the row between the Apostles Peter and Paul, which Paul wrote about in his letter to the Galatians. Evidently some Jewish leaders felt that since they were the chosen people from whom Christianity evolved, any gentile who wanted to become a Christian first had to become a Jew by being circumcised and observing the Mosaic rites. Peter was of this opinion but Paul was not and, as Paul wrote the Galatians: "When Peter came to Antioch, I withstood him to his face because he was to be blamed." That must have been quite a sight, those two tremendous, powerful men standing there toe to toe.

Paul asked Peter: "If you, a Jew, are now living like the gentiles and not like the Jews, why are you compelling the gentiles to live like the Jews?" Peter's answer was not recorded, probably because Paul didn't give him a chance to get a word in. But Paul was undoubtedly in the right, and He quoted both the Father and the Son to prove it. God had chosen the Jews as His people primarily to provide the lineage which would produce the beautiful young woman who would become the virgin mother of the Saviour of the world. God told Abraham: "In thee shall all nations be blessed." And Jesus ordered His disciples: "Go ye forth and teach all nations." Salvation, then, was not to be limited to the chosen people alone.

A conflict of opinion is not a bad thing in itself. It is the resolution of the conflict that makes the difference. At ServiceMaster we have a conflict of opinions even on the matter of religion. We have people working with us of many denominations, and though we agree on essentials we have different attitudes regarding the particulars. But we have enough respect for each other to be able to view the particulars as personal matters, and so we are able to get together in the conference room on Friday mornings to sing and pray together as we enjoy the fellowship that has made us a team.

It has become a ServiceMaster custom for me to give the opening talk at our regional conferences around the country each year, and I use these opportunities to remind the men of our company's philosophy. A few years ago, an associate of another faith let me know that he sometimes found my talks personally offensive. I told him I was sorry to hear that and I suggested we discuss it. I reminded him that he had looked us over before coming with us, had learned how we operated and had seemed anxious enough to join the organization. I pointed out that we hadn't changed, so perhaps he had. Then I told him what I do in such situations. When I'm reading anything that becomes offensive to me, I throw it out; when I find something on television offensive, I switch channels or turn off the set; when I'm with people whose conduct becomes offensive, I excuse myself. Then I said: "If you find my talks offensive, I won't mind if you leave the room, but if you find the company's policies offensive maybe you ought to leave the firm. I know you're doing a good job, so I hope you'll stay. I know you've got your convictions, but remember that I have mine. As long as we both live up to them, we can work together." He agreed, and we're still working together.

When men live their Christian faith they can work out any conflict to their mutual satisfaction and self-respect. In the Bible, we can see conflict between men whose religion was their work. Paul and Barnabas had a conflict when Barnabas wanted to take his nephew along on a missionary trip, and when they couldn't settle the matter Barnabas said: "All right, Paul, you take one road and Mark and I will take another. We'll all get more work done for the Lord that way, anyway." And they did. Paul expressed his satisfaction with the compromise in various letters.

The Saviour Himself encountered conflict of opinions. When He wanted John the Baptist to baptize Him,

John backed away and said: "You should baptize me, not I You." But Jesus said: "Do it now, for thus it becomes us to fulfill all righteousness." On another occasion, Jesus surprised the Apostles by indicating that He was about to wash their feet. Peter was really astonished, and he said: "Lord, You are not about to wash my feet, are You?" And Jesus said: "Peter, you don't know everything yet. I have a purpose in doing this." He went on to explain that He expected all of them to be willing to wash each other's feet, that by this act of humility they would remember that the servant was not greater than the master, and that He was not greater than the Father who had sent Him.

We can never know the Lord's purpose for putting us in certain situations but as long as we follow Him trustingly we can be sure that the purpose is good, either for us or someone else. I had an experience some years ago that led me to believe that the Lord has used me for His purposes. A supplier with whom we did business had made a mistake on an estimate, leaving himself in a position to suffer a sizable loss. When we learned of this, our people re-negotiated the contract and he was able to salvage something. As he was leaving the building he stopped at my office to thank me and to express his high opinion of the way the men had handled the problem. He said that nobody else had ever treated him as fairly as our men had, and he was grateful.

I asked him: "Do you know why they did business that way?"

"Because they're nice people, I suppose," he answered.

"Well, that's one of the reasons," I said, "but it goes a little deeper than that. Do you have a few minutes?"

We sat down and I explained why and how Service-Master operated as it did. From his comments, I perceived that he had little acquantance with the Bible. He knew about the Golden Rule and the Sermon on the Mount, but that was about it. He admitted he didn't read the Bible, so I picked up mine and showed him several reasons why I did. Before he left, he made a profession for Christ there in my office, and he became a Christian. Some time later, he told me about an executives' club he belonged to, suggesting that it might be good for my business if I joined. He warned me that the members occasionally got a little rough in their humor, but he said the best way for me to determine if I wanted to join was to attend a luncheon as his guest. We made a date for the following week.

I arrived at the luncheon with two guests of my own. The previous day, as a result of a radio talk I gave, a New Yorker in town came to see me. A new Christian, he had a couple of problems he felt I could help him with. My calendar was full, so I invited him to the lunch, suggesting we talk after it. The other man, a close friend and a Christian gentleman, happened to be free for lunch when I stopped in to visit on the way to the appointment, so I invited him, too. With our host, we sat at a table for eight, and one of the other men there decided to start the sociability with some dirty jokes. They didn't go over, and the man was puzzled because he obviously thought they were funny. Without malice, the New Yorker said: "A year ago I would have laughed at that, but I've become a Christian and I just can't see the humor in it any more." This didn't help much and I could see we were developing a situation, so I moved in with a few of my own jokes. They were good and they were clean, and once everybody got laughing we were able to forget that man's unfortunate effort to establish the same friendly atmosphere.

After lunch, my host said: "Well, it's pretty obvious that you wouldn't want to become a member of this group."

I said: "No, that's not true. I've met some fine men today and they've certainly tried to be friendly. You told me that if I join the club I'll have an opportunity to give a talk about my business and what it means to me. I think this is a good place for that, so put up my name."

A few weeks later I was at the head table, telling my story. I didn't pull any punches, explaining that the goal of ServiceMaster was to honor God in the marketplace, to show that it could be done and to persuade others to give it a try. Judging from complimentary comments in the next club bulletin, the talk was viewed as being sincere. So I was in the group. Almost immediately I began to receive a number of calls from new customers who said ServiceMaster had been recommended by a member of the club, a man who was in the liquor business.

I thanked the man at the next meeting, and as the calls kept coming in I finally had to tell him: "Friend, you've really got me over a barrel. I feel like a big heel because you've been recommending me and I'm getting some fine business through you but I can't recommend your business to anybody because I'm against it. I don't drink and I certainly wouldn't recommend it to anybody else. I feel badly about it, but that's the situation."

He laughed and said: "You don't have to feel badly, I've given up drinking myself. And as a matter of fact I'm thinking seriously of getting out of the business."

I could have argued with that man until I was blue in the face and never have persuaded him to get out of his business. I didn't know then—and I don't know now—how much influence my talk had on his decision but I do believe it was the work of God that he and I were in the same room the day I gave it. And I believe something else. It was a direct result of the way my host had been treated by ServiceMaster people that he became a Christian. This is the way we at ServiceMaster ask the Lord to use our company—to help bring others to Him. We remained friends for years. Recently when I learned of his sudden death from a heart attack I had the consolation of knowing that my friend had gone to be with the Lord.

Paul, in explaining himself to the Corinthians, said:

For I am the least of the apostles, that am not meet to be called an apostle, because I persecuted the church of God.

But by the grace of God I am what I am: and his grace which *was bestowed* upon me was not in vain; but I laboured more abundantly than they all: yet not I, but the grace of God which was with me.

(I Cor. 15:9, 10.) In other words, Paul felt that the good he was doing was actually being done by God through him. The good we do, then, is God's good, and when we surrender ourselves to Him we are letting Him use us for His own needs. It was the Lord who got through to those two men. It was the Lord who set up the whole situation. I was merely the means to His end.

Can a man know when he is being used by the Lord? Not always. But if he conscientiously lives according to the Bible he can be sure that sooner or later, in one way or another, the Lord will use him because he is dependable. Is it spiritual vanity to believe that the Creator of Heaven and earth and all things desires the cooperation of an ordinary, mortal man to carry out His will? The person who believes in the Bible knows that this desire of God's is an everyday occurrence. When the Lord knocked Paul, the persecutor, off his horse, Paul caught on fast and immediately asked: "Lord, what wilt thou have me do?" Is it spiritual vanity, then, for an ordinary man to put himself in Paul's class? On the contrary, everything in the Bible represents something we should or should not do, according to the context, and to feel that any part of it doesn't pertain to each of us specifically is hypocrisy, stupidity or false humility.

Assuming that a man isn't stupid, the only remaining issue to be resolved is: Is he honest? Is he truthful with the Lord, with himself, with other people? On the face of it, it seems ridiculous to try to be dishonest with the Lord, who sees right into our hearts. But when a man is being dishonest with himself, living by his personal double standard, he is also being dishonest with the Lord, trying to hide things from Him, and he knows this even when he won't admit it. In Galatians 6:7 is the warning: "Be not deceived; God is not mocked: for whatsoever a man soweth, that shall he also reap." This, too, is something that a lot of people don't bother to think about much as they battle through life concerned only with Number One.

Often when two men are involved in a conflict of opinion, the basic problem is that one of them doesn't know the truth or won't accept it. According to the dictionary, truth is the state or character of being true in relation to being, knowledge or speech. And according to the same dictionary, the word true has some illuminating synonyms: authentic, faithful, good, honest, just, moral, right, pure. These are Bible words if ever I heard any. They apply even to the famous argument between Peter and Paul regarding circumcision and the Mosaic Law. Peter had taken on the job of evangelizing the Jews, and apparently some of his prominent converts, being perhaps a bit too proud of their history, had influenced his thinking to the point where his attitude could not be described by the aforementioned synonyms. Paul, who was working among the gentiles, straightened Peter out by quoting the Scriptures and Peter came around.

Both the Old and New Testaments instruct us about truthfulness. The prophet Zechariah said: "These are the things that ye shall do: Speak ye every man truth to his neighbor; execute the judgment of truth and peace in your gates." And Paul told the Ephesians: "Speak every man truth with his neighbor, for we are members of one another." And John reports Jesus Christ as saying: "I am the way, the truth, and the life: no man cometh unto the Father, but by me." That is about as plain as it can be put.

But as Amos once remarked to Andy: "In da big print dey gives it to ya, and in da little print dey takes it all away." It is sadly true that many businesses juggle their responsibilities in this way, though most of the time they don't put it into print. The customer's surprise comes when it's time for the pay-off. Also, it's been said that a liar better have a good memory, and this is another sad truth. Even worse, the double-dealer, the fast operator, the truth juggler is going to sink lower and lower in the mire until he gets trapped by his own tricks, and a lot of innocent people get hurt.

The Saviour said to His followers: "And ye shall know the truth, and the truth shall make you free." (John 8:32.) Here is the wonderful reward of truthfulness: the freedom of mind and soul. The truthful businessman doesn't have to waste his brains trying to straighten out his maze of past lies; he can be free to use his intellect as God meant him to—creatively. The business leader who is truthful with his ads, his labels and his contracts is free from worry whenever he gets a letter from some Federal agency. Men of conflicting opinions can hassle all day, free of the fear of being truthful, as long as it's the truth they're after. All men can go through life free of any dread of retribution in this world or the next when they know the truth and live it.

One man who couldn't recognize the truth was Pontius Pilate, when the Lord was brought before him for judgment. Though Jesus Christ never claimed the title King of the Jews, some of his ardent followers gave it to Him. And so His enemies were able to take Him before Pilate on charges of being a political insurgent who was trying to overthrow the Roman conquerors. Pilate asked Him: "Are you the King of the Jews?"

Jesus answered: "Are you asking me this for your own satisfaction or because others have said this of me to you?"

Pilate got a little impatient, and he asked: "Am I a Jew? Do you think it makes any difference to me who claims to be King of the Jews? The Romans are in charge here. The point is that your own people and the chief priest have delivered you to me for judgment. Now, what have you done?"

The Lord said: "My kingdom is not of this world. If my kingdom were of this world, then my followers would rise up and fight so that I should not be delivered to the Jews. But my kingdom is not from here."

Pilate thought this over a moment, then asked: "Are you saying, then, that you really are a king?"

"You are the one who is saying that," said Jesus. "To this end was I born and for this cause came I into the world, that I should bear witness to the truth. Everyone who is of the truth hears my voice."

Pilate, who had been raised in a pagan, materialistic society where truth was whatever anybody wanted to make it, cynically asked: "What is truth?"

The Eternal Truth incarnate was at that moment standing right in front of him. Every day He stands in front of each one of us and invites: "Come, follow Me."

... 10 ...

LOVE CASTS OUT FEAR
—EVEN OF COMPETITION

One day while Sam Snead, the golf champion, was competing in a Midwest tournament (so the story goes), a fellow stepped up to him in the clubhouse and, hoping to get a little free advice, said: "Mr. Snead, I'd like to ask you a couple of questions about improving my game." Snead said: "I charge twenty-five dollars a question." The fellow asked: "That's pretty steep, isn't it?" And Snead said: "Yes, it is. Now, what's your other question?"

That is one of the most practical examples of a realistic businessman that I have ever heard. I can appreciate it because I try to be practical and realistic with my business, and I have found I can also be practical and realistic with my religion. The Bible has given me clear instructions on how to do this.

For example, the third time the Saviour appeared to His disciples after His resurrection was on the shores of the Sea of Tiberias. The men had been out fishing all night and without any luck at all. Early in the morning someone standing on the shore called out to them: "Young men, have you caught anything?" They shouted back that they hadn't, and the person on shore said: "Cast your nets on the right side of the ship and you shall find." Over the side went the nets again, and this time they came up loaded.

It was at this point that John, the beloved disciple and author of the Fourth Gospel, took a closer look at the man on the shore, then said to Peter: "It is the Lord!" Everybody took a close look and, sure enough, it was He. I often wonder what these men felt at that moment, especially John, who had been the only disciple to stand at the foot of the Cross on Calvary. They all knew Jesus had died; they all knew He had been buried; they knew, too, that He had risen, and now they were seeing Him again. This staggering experience imbued these men with the faith that later enabled them to face violent death for His sake, because they believed in Him. The Lord hasn't asked such sacrifices of many people since then, but He has asked us to have the same faith. When we become better acquainted with these men by reading the Bible, the faith comes easier and clearer.

Obviously, the Lord didn't repeatedly appear to the disciples after His resurrection because He had no better place to go. He knew that His work wasn't finished, and each time He appeared He had a special point to get across. This time, after the disciples had come ashore and they all had breakfast, the Lord asked Peter: "Simon, son of Jonas, lovest thou me more than these?" Peter said: "Yea, Lord, Thou knowest that I love Thee." And Jesus said: "Feed my lambs." The Lord was so determined to make His point clear that He asked Peter the same question two more times, and when Peter admitted that he loved the Lord, He said again: "Feed my lambs. . . . Feed my sheep."

Who are the lambs? Who are the sheep? We are— the Christian flock. The brethren. And the Good Shepherd said we are to feed the flock. We are to take care of each other. We are to care. This commandment applies to the business world as well as everywhere else.

When a man really knows his Bible he has learned that whenever the Lord asks something of us He is always ready to be more than generous in return. He said: "Give, and it shall be given unto you; good measure, pressed down, and shaken together, and running over shall men give into your bosom. For with the same measure that ye mete withal it shall be measured to you again." (Luke 6: 38.) There is an extraordinary promise in those words, which can be interpreted as: "Conduct your business as I have told you and don't worry about what the other fellow might do to you, for I shall take care of you." Remember, this wasn't the Better Business Bureau speaking. It was the Saviour of the world. We're always quick to remember His offer: "Ask and ye shall receive." Occasionally we remember to thank Him when He makes good on the offer. But when it comes to what

He asks of us, when He tells us how to run our companies, we shake our heads and say He must be kidding.

In addition to telling Christians take care of each other, the Lord specifically instructed us to love each other, and it might help if men had a better understanding of love. A man experiences different kinds of love, toward his parents, his wife, his children, his relatives, his friends, his community, his country, his hobbies, his pets, his work. Each love has its own expressions, its own laws; each love has its own set of tracks on which it travels toward the greatest love, God. Love is not merely an emotion or an affection. Love is devotion in motion. It has to go somewhere; it has to do something; it must be fulfilled according to the nature of the relationship, and the fulfillment should be in terms of the Lord. The love that stands still is like the ad for a new bath soap, which read: "It won't float. It won't lather. It won't smell. It won't clean. It just keeps you company."

If in business the competition is the enemy, then the Lord has commanded us how to conduct ourselves: Do good. An example of this occurred in Chicago a few years ago. One of our newspapers had a fire that burned out the pressroom. Few day-to-day businesses are as highly competitive as newspaper publishing and, in modern terms, I suppose, other publishers could have gloated and said: "Good. That paper won't be on the stands for a long time. Now let's grab as many of its readers as we can and keep them with us." Instead, every other paper in town offered its presses to the burned-out publisher and he was able to stay in business without missing an issue. It was as though the others were saying: "We'd like to get some of your customers but we want to win them over by putting out a better paper than yours, not by taking advantage of your hard luck."

It is a sad commentary on American business that this kind of friendly competition on the basis of quality does not widely prevail. In some businesses, it wouldn't be unlikely for somebody to go over to the other fellow's place and start the fire. Many businessmen virtually go that far when they try to get ahead by setting fire to the competition's reputation by backstabbing and conniving.

Admittedly, it is usually difficult to fraternize with competitors because of the undercurrent of animosity which generally exists, but the animosity exists mainly because of the way a lot of people do business. When the business emphasis is on the quality of the product and the service, the fiercest competitors can nevertheless be as close as brothers. It is when a man starts cutting corners in order to cut prices and thereby undersell the competition that the thing gets dirty. Competitors can respect each other only when each man has self-respect, and there can't be much self-respect in a company that is operating at the level of prostitution. "Love your neighbor as you love yourself," the Saviour commanded, putting this and the love of God even above the Ten Commandments. The man who truly loves his neighbor and truly loves God won't have any trouble with the Commandments because he has freed himself from the temptation to break them. Any baseball fan knows that there isn't much of the "After you, Alphonse" spirit in a pennant play-off, but it is common knowledge that players on opposing teams are often close friends with a lot of respect for each other. When you respect a competitor for what he does well you're not only able to get along with him better but you can learn from him how to improve your own game, and then the goal of the competition becomes winning the league pennant instead of trying to force each other into bankruptcy.

The Bible says: "To know to do good and not do it is sin." *Do good*, then, means more than *Don't do evil.* Not doing evil can mean not doing anything, and this is what the Lord specifically condemned when He criticized people for being lukewarm about their religion. The Bible tells us that we must actually go out and actively do good. Jesus Christ explained this in His story about the king who wanted to reprimand some of his people. The king said:

> For I was an hungred, and ye gave me no meat: I was thirsty, and ye gave me no drink:
> I was a stranger, and ye took me not in: naked, and ye clothed me not: sick, and in prison, and ye visited me not.
> Then shall they also answer him, saying, Lord, when saw we thee an hungred, or athirst, or a stranger, or naked, or sick, or in prison, and did not minister unto thee?
> Then shall he answer them, saying, Verily I say unto you,

Inasmuch as ye did *it* not to one of the least of these, ye did *it* not to me.

And these shall go away into everlasting punishment: but the righteous into life eternal.

(Matt. 25:42-46.) The puzzled people looked at each other and then at the king and they asked: "When did all this happen?" The king said: "Inasmuch as you have not done these things for the least of my brethren you have not done them for me." When we neglect to do good, then, or when we refuse to do good, we are neglecting and refusing the Lord. And when doing good we're not supposed to play favorites, but we must do good for all the brethren.

We are at a point in history where our survival as a nation no longer depends on military power or national wealth but rather on the individual conduct of every citizen in the land. We are confronted by a group of countries which have cut themselves off from God, openly, boldly, boastfully. In an effort to advance materially, they have rejected Christian morality as the yardstick of their ways and means. Their leaders deny God before the world. Their astronauts return to earth with the cynical news that they didn't see any angels out there. Derisively they are saying: "See how much we have accomplished in a short time without the help of the God on whom the capitalists say they depend so much. And we've just started. Soon we will leave the Americans and their God in the dust."

The terrifying part of it all is that they just might do it, and if so it will happen because too many Americans have already left God in the dust when it comes to make moral judgments in the areas of their lives for which they are morally responsible. Our national motto—In God We Trust—which appears many times in the Bible has been replaced by "The Lord helps those who help themselves," which doesn't appear in the Bible at all. Technology and progress have become our national religion. Comfort and luxury have become our national goals. Clever lawyers have become more important than devout preachers.

Psalm 127 begins: "Except the Lord build the house, they labor in vain that built it: except the Lord keep the city, the watchman waketh in vain." Now, either that is true or it isn't, and if it isn't then we might as well forget the whole thing and go right ahead and try to beat the Communists at their own game. If the Communists intended to remain inside their own domain, we wouldn't have to worry about them so much. But they are out to convert the world, either by war or persuasion. Today they are busiest where Christianity is weakest—in Africa and the Far East—and they are goading these people to revolutions with the materialistic bait of wealth and power. Strangely enough, this same bait seems to be the only appeal we are offering these people to bring them our way.

Let us remember that the Pilgrims who first settled this country came here in search of religious freedom.

Let us also remember that the men who wrote the Declaration of Independence, the Constitution and the Bill of Rights were religious men. Let us remember, too, that religion was so much in the minds of early Americans that even the dates of such national events as Election Day and Inauguration Day were chosen because they were less apt to fall on a Sunday—the Sabbath which the people so piously observed that they would not desecrate it even to perform their duties as citizens. Let us remember these things. Let us teach them to our children. Let's all live by them. We have already drifted too far away from the basic principles on which this nation was built. In a Communist country these days, a child can have his father put in jail by reporting him to the authorities if he makes any remark that is critical of the government. God forbid that this should ever happen in America, but so many things are happening that never occurred before that one wonders.

Without any doubt, the greatness of America has evolved from the simple fact that because of the religious spirit of our forefathers the Lord did build the house and has kept watch over the city. There is no other explanation for it. And the only explanation for the downfall of America would be the sad fact that we had turned our backs on God and rejected His will as He has revealed it in the Bible. And we would have lost by default. We must not let this happen.

Today America may be at the top of the heap, but we are not at the end of the road. Life still demands that mountains be moved, water be walked on and the impossible be accomplished. The place America has achieved in history has not served to make our lives easier but rougher, for the more a man has the greater is his responsibility for it. We are now at a point on the road when our responsibilities are greater than ever and we are more in need of miracles than man has been in all his centuries on this planet. If, as we make our personal and business decisions in our daily life, we continue our abandonment of God, the maker of miracles, then we are sunk. Our only hope is the assurance that Lord still stands by ready to help us. These are His own words: (John 15: 1-8)

> I am the true vine, and my Father is the husbandman.
> Every branch in me that beareth not fruit he taketh away: and every *branch* that beareth fruit, he purgeth it, that it may bring forth more fruit.
> Now Ye are clean through the word which I have spoken unto you.
> Abide in me, and I in you. As the branch cannot bear fruit of itself, except it abide in the vine; no more can ye, except ye abide in me.
> I am the vine, ye *are* the branches: He that abideth in me, and I in him, the same bringeth forth much fruit: for without me ye can do nothing.
> If a man abide not in me, he is cast forth as a branch, and is withered; and men gather them, and they are burned.
> If ye abide in me, and my words abide in you, ye shall ask what ye will, and it shall be done unto you.
> Herein is my Father glorified, that ye bear much fruit; so shall ye be my disciples.

A Christian, then, is a disciple of Christ and must go to work for Christ, starting with himself. "Be ye perfect as the Father is perfect," Jesus said. And if that sounds like an impossibility we need only remember that Paul told the Romans that those who accept Christ and live Christ will be, like Him, lifted up by the Holy Spirit and that "as many as are led by the Spirit of God, they are the sons of God. . . . The Spirit itself beareth witness with our spirit, that we are the children of God: And if children, then heirs, heirs of God, and the joint-heirs with Christ; if so be that we suffer with Him, that we may also be glorified together."

While working at his own discipleship, the Christian has also been ordered to make disciples of others. According to recent statistics, there are about 3.5 billion people in the world, of whom some 950 million are Christians—around 33 percent. On the one hand, it is amazing to realize that this tremendous spiritual revolution began when eleven men walked across the city limits of Jerusalem to start telling others about the Lord. On the other hand, it must be admitted that if all of today's Christians were really working at it that percentage would shoot up overnight.

Christians have a mandate to fulfill, and its terms are clearly set forth in God's word—the Bible. Certainly it was not by accident or even through men's best efforts that the Bible has survived for thousands of years and in spite of many attempts to destroy it. Other ancient documents, some packed with more complete historical details, have disappeared. Obviously God gave us the Bible, He has protected it, and the only way men lose it is when they don't use it. Today, by neglecting it, men can lose everything else.

The entire situation boils down to two questions:

1. Does the businessman have to make a choice between God and man?

2. Though executives have demonstrated that they can control the technical problems of business, why haven't they been able to control the moral problems?

The Bible has the answers.

1. In Matthew 6:24, the Lord says: "No man can serve two masters: for either he will hate the one, and love the other; or else he will hold to the one, and despise the other. Ye cannot serve God and mammon." Therefore, the businessman must make a choice. If he has any spiritual consciousness at all, he will choose God, and he will serve God by using the Bible as the handbook for his relations with men.

2. In Corinthians 2:14, Paul says: "The natural men receiveth not the things of the Spirit of God, for they are foolishness unto him. Neither can he know them because they are spiritually discerned." In other words, unless a man himself is of the spirit he will not understand the things of the spirit. They simply won't get through to him. He will be in the hopeless position of the truck driver on a narrow country road who kept holding up traffic by getting out his truck every few

minutes, going around to the side and hitting it with a stick. Finally the driver behind him asked what on earth he was doing, and he explained: "I've got a one-ton truck and I've got two tons of canary birds in there, so I have to keep half of them in the air."

The natural man can read the Bible all day long and not get anything out of it. He can't apply the Bible to the moral problems in his business because, first, he isn't sure what morality is and, second, by his naturalness he has built a wall around himself. If he wants to change this, he has to be reborn, he must become of the spirit. Whether he does it in his living room, at his desk or at an altar, he must make a declaration for Christ, a deliberate and conscious acceptance of Jesus Christ as Lord and Saviour. When he does this, when he becomes of the spirit, he is indeed reborn, for his senses seem to come alive in a new way. The things of the spirit to which he was deaf, dumb and blind before can now reach into his mind, his heart and his soul. He now regards the Bible as the spiritual nourishment he needs to keep himself alive, and he bears witness to his rebirth by applying the Bible to his daily affairs. That's all there is to it, but without it there is nothing at all.

Each one of us came into this world alone and each one of us will go out of it alone. If there is nothing more to life than the few years we have here, then mankind is no better off than animal creation. But it is my belief that God has always wanted men to have a Heaven, that this is why He started the human race, why He sent His

177

Son to win Heaven for us, and why He gave us the Bible as a lasting testament of the way to reach it. It is the way open to any man who has ever lived. When we refuse to enter it and follow its course, we not only throw away our life but we throw away our Heaven as well.

When I was a boy in Arkansas, the only doctor in our town was old Doc Hamil, who made no secret of his lack of religious convictions. When I was four, I developed pneumonia, and the night of the crisis my appendix ruptured. Doc Hamil took one look at me and told my mother that I would be dead before morning. But when he returned in the morning I was still here and practically recovered. After examining me, Doc Hamil shook his head and said to my mother: "Well, Mrs. Wade, I'm not a Christian, but the only explanation for this is that the Lord must have something for this boy to do."

Perhaps I have done it in writing this book.